everything

that is

not a

belief

is

true

everything

that is

not a

belief

is

true

Ray Menezes

Matador
9 Priory Business Park,
Wistow Road, Kibworth Beauchamp,
Leicestershire. LE8 0RX
Tel: (+44) 116 279 2299
Fax: (+44) 116 279 2277
Email: books@troubador.co.uk
Web: www.troubador.co.uk/matador

ISBN 978 1780880 464

British Library Cataloguing in Publication Data.
A catalogue record for this book is available from the British Library.

Typeset in 11pt Adobe Garamond Pro by Troubador Publishing Ltd, Leicester, UK
Printed and bound in Great Britain by TJ International Ltd, Padstow, Cornwall

Matador is an imprint of Troubador Publishing Ltd

For help with editing Yvonne Dixon.
Front Cover photograph 'Magical Morning' from Petri Volanen.
My dear friend Ishi for his poem Salutation to the Sat Guru.

Contents

Please do not read this if you wish to retain your false beliefs.

Sooner or later, all false beliefs must end in suffering.

Without belief, there are no teachers, gurus or gods.

Do not assume that 'reality' without beliefs is cold, heartless, unloving, uncaring, pointless, meaningless, nihilistic or any other negatives. All of these are beliefs.

Saying something is so does not make it so – it either is or is not so. If it is so it can never be contained or described.

Belief always has an agenda; find out what that agenda is.

The absence of belief would be very bad for business, be that worldly or spiritual business.

Illness is often the body's response to false beliefs. This is truer still of most mental illness.

The absence of belief is the end of all suffering – suffering here is defined as believing that which is untrue.

Whatever you believe is what you become. Belief in this sense is the same as neurosis, psychosis, hate, fear, anxiety, depression, desire and, of course, 'awakening'.

The absence of belief is not to be feared as fear cannot and does not exist without belief.

Belief is a prop to replace the truth.

Belief is dead before it is born.

Without belief, who are you and who is anyone else?

Without belief, what is life and death?

The mind is likely to throw up immense fear and doubt when faced with the end of all beliefs. Fear and doubt are also beliefs.

Find out for yourself what happens when belief ends.

Instructions for working with belief – absolutely none, as all instructions can only arise from more beliefs.

Instructions for reading this – do not use this to construct new beliefs.

These words will act as a virus until all false beliefs are annihilated.

Do not think that without beliefs you can do what you want (negative deeds). It is only with beliefs that this could occur.

Thoughts are beliefs; rather than trying to get rid of thought, see the truth that all beliefs are untrue.

Thoughts naturally arise and pass away, as do all things. If they are not invested with meaning (belief) when they arise they quickly and naturally pass away.

Belief is the ego's attempt to justify its own existence. As the ego does not in fact exist, this attempt is doomed to failure.

If you believe anything that is untrue, then it is likely that you will feel disturbed if you hear anything that threatens this belief. Feeling threatened is a sure sign that you believe something that is untrue.

Salutation to the Sat Guru

Frustration, disgust, despair
The mighty triumvirate
Through which the Sat Guru brings one
To his knees

Frustration,
Because Samsara never delivers the goods
Not that which is hoped for
Nor shelter from that which is feared
While Kali Ma (death) gleefully looks on
Waiting for the last dance

Disgust,
Because Ego and his daughter Time
Can do nothing about it

Hope and Fear
These are the twin sisters
That keep Ego busy striving
On the treadmill going nowhere
Also known as Samsara (cyclic existence)

Frustration, disgust, despair
These are the excellent agents
The Sat Guru's own inherent awareness uses
To bring one home
Who am I?

Sat, Chit, Anand
Existence, consciousness, bliss
No center, no circumference
No inside, no outside

Frustration becomes insight
Disgust matures into determination to be free
And despair gives way to sweet surrender
Hari Om Sat Guru Dev

Ishi

1. The Finger that Points at the Moon

All that you may think, speak, believe, or conceive of is false. 'False' in this sense means unrelated to anything that is. All that is surrounds you now and, without thinking, it still is. Even when we think about it, it still is, but now we have inadvertently created a problem. This problem is superimposed over what is. The superimposition may be composed of 'I like' or 'I don't like' or an infinity of other beliefs, none of which have any relationship to what is. The fact that we do not see the false as false is the reason behind every problem in the world.

This is very easy to check. In any given conflict, is anything being believed? This is of course very obvious how could there be a conflict without a belief? It is not that one belief is better or worse than another belief, it is that all beliefs are false. The reason why this is so difficult to accept is because usually we have the mistaken assumption that without some kind of belief we would be unable to do anything or that we would enter some kind of vegetative state. These are just more beliefs and are absolutely untrue.

How do we know if a thing is true or not? As far as most people are concerned, there is only one way that we can know if a thing is true or not; we have to believe something. If you did not believe in something, it would be unnecessary to know if something is true or not. In fact, without belief the question would not even arise. The answer to the question 'how do we know if a thing is true or not' is we cannot know we can only believe.

A Zen koan is a problem that cannot be answered using the ego; there is a solution, but not one that the ego could ever arrive at. It could be said that life itself is a koan and most people are trying to solve this koan using the ego – the ego being that which thinks and conceives.

My favourite Zen koan is 'believing neither good nor evil right now, what is my true nature?' This is not just a question; it is both the question and the answer.

The first part of the koan can be translated as 'believing nothing'; understanding this part that anything that can be conceived of in any way is inherently untrue makes the second part of the koan redundant. Any belief whatsoever about your true nature is stated to be false. The beauty of this koan is that it is indicating that your true nature is not something you could ever conceive of or understand.

What are the implications of all this? It seems that when hearing something like this, our mind again arrives at certain conclusions such as 'I can understand that some of the things we think and believe are not true, but this can't mean all of them'. But this conclusion leaves us exactly where we started, which is what most people believe; some things are true and some are false. Each one of us decides which category our beliefs fall into.

The key thing about all beliefs being false is that without your beliefs you collapse, and when you collapse what is left is truth. As long as any beliefs are held, we can only exist as a lie. The beliefs themselves are a lie, but any belief that suggests there is a 'someone' who believes something is the biggest lie of all.

Everything stated so far is also untrue, and this produces a very interesting question. If nothing I say can be held as true, why say anything? This question needs to be asked of all 'spiritual' teachings of the past, present, or future. Some teachers seem to be aware that what is being said is clearly untrue.

For instance, in Zen it is said that 'the finger that points at the moon is not the moon', and that 'in the beginning a mountain is a mountain, and then it is not a mountain, and then it is a mountain again'. Here, the word 'finger' represents the idea that the thing that points and that which is pointed at are entirely different things. The finger that points is the same as the words you are reading right now. The moon is that which is there prior to any pointing. This idea has immense significance in the world as so many people believe what they are told or read and then act on those beliefs. Sometimes they are even prepared to kill or do harm for those beliefs.

'In the beginning, a mountain is a mountain and then it is not a mountain, and then it is a mountain again' refers to the idea that, prior to naming or conceiving of 'mountain', the thing that we call 'mountain' exists. Then, when we name and conceive of 'mountain', it no longer exists for us it has now become a name and a concept. The last part 'and then it is a mountain again' is a completion of a process that we all have to go through, to get back to the truth that the word and the concept have no relationship to the thing itself.

All pain has its root in the belief in something that is not true. This principle operates on many levels. One level concerns external reality. For instance, jumping out of a window believing that if you flap your arms hard enough you will fly is clearly a false belief and one that could be very dangerous.

Another similar belief could be, 'I believe that someone whom I love loves me'. This belief could turn out to be true or untrue. If this belief is found to be untrue, the result could be experienced as painful the pain in this instance is only telling us that something we believed to be true is not true.

There are so many of these beliefs about external reality that we could spend our entire life experiencing the pain of every belief that is not true. Fortunately, there is one belief we have that is not true that cuts through every other belief in a single swipe – the belief that all other beliefs rest upon is that belief itself is somehow meaningful. As soon as it is seen that belief itself is the only problem we have ever had, there is freedom. This is the freedom from our own beliefs.

Seeing in the sense I am referring to is the same as the seeing involved when I touch something very hot. There is no belief involved in this seeing, only a very deep knowing that demands action.

2. Mystery

Before every thought, before every action and before every bodily sensation lies the mystery at the centre of our being. This mystery is all that we seek, even though we appear to be seeking for something else. This mystery cannot be found, because to search for it would imply that it is lost. The mystery is all that we really are; all that is, is also the mystery.

The act of looking at the world distracts us from this mystery. Believing myself to be something or someone distracts me from the mystery. All that is arises from the mystery. There is nothing outside of the mystery. The mystery is not subject to time or space in fact, there is no time or space as these are concepts invented to distract ourselves from the mystery. All that is contained in the whole of time and space is also invented as a distraction from the mystery.

Whether we know it or not, we are all searching for something. This something could be money, power, love, sex, drugs, food or happiness. When we attain or approach any of these, we feel for a while that we are closer to the thing we are searching for. We are no closer to the thing we are searching for, but we may be closer to a necessary sense of futility; that no matter what we attain, it is never enough, and sooner or later the search continues – always with the same result.

In the world of ego, all roads lead to futility. Buddhism refers to this as the unsatisfactory nature of desire; wanting something with the mistaken idea that once attained this something will produce happiness in us. This is possible, but for how long does the happiness last? We all know the answer to this question; it does not last. Sometimes, the moment the desired object is attained the mind is already looking for the next object to pursue. I am not saying that we should not eat, have sex, or earn money. The particular point I am making is that something always goes wrong when we do anything with the idea that attaining what we desire will make us happy. In this process, we always find that we are looking in the wrong direction.

Anything that is subject to change cannot lead to permanence or happiness. What is subject to change? This list is endless; all things except one are subject to change and even this one thing that is not, cannot be named or described in any way – and yet it exists. Infuriating, isn't it?

This is the way it is. It does not matter if you believe it or not. Life will always present you with many wonderful objects of desire and life will always take those objects away, because all things with the exception of one are subject to change. The point is that if you desire anything that is subject to change, you will lose it.

So how are we to find the one thing that is not subject to change? This seems incredibly difficult; it is like looking for a needle in a billion haystacks. It is even more difficult than that, because if you are looking for it, this also means you will fail. It will fail because the one who is looking is subject to change. If you are feeling a sense of futility in all this, then you are on the right track; you just need now to amplify this futility until there is no hope whatsoever. This is not something you can do, but it is something you are being led towards, another reason why you cannot find it is because finding implies that it is lost, which it is not.

When we desire something, we either lose consciousness, become unconscious, or dream while appearing to be wide awake. When the futility of desire reaches a critical level, the whole show collapses, revealing the one thing that is not subject to change. If something is conceivable, it is subject to change. Let us take the notion of God and ask is this subject to change? You may believe in God in a particular way now, but this can and will change. You might conceive of a God that is not subject to change, but the one who conceived of this God is subject to change. Because he is subject to change, he will change. In fact, at no point does God exist except as a notion or a conception.

Clearly, concepts can and do change, but they do not exist as anything actual in the first place. See if you can find something that is not subject to change.

Take however long you need to do this but remember that whatever you find must be a concept and therefore is subject to change. I am not saying that God or anything else does not exist, but that anything conceptual cannot exist because it can only point towards something that may or may not be actual.

3. Desire

Desire can never be for that which I already have, it can only be for that which I believe I am lacking. The belief that who you are is not complete is a false belief and yet it does relate to something that must lead you towards that which is true. Believing that I am incomplete, I am compelled to search for that which will complete me. If you are human, then you are searching for that which will complete you. This was true for the Buddha, or Jesus or any other human who ever lived. What all of these past teachers found was not something that completed them, but that this belief that they needed completing was false.

The journey we take to arrive at this truth must therefore be necessary. Even though we are searching for something that was never missing, we are compelled to search. The nature of reality is such that anything you find that is subject to change means that whatever you find will fall away until even the belief that there is something to find will fall away.

Believing that you have lost a necklace, you search everywhere to find it until eventually someone points out that it is not lost, it is hanging around your neck. In this case, someone else can see what we cannot see; that the necklace was never lost. Seeing us frantically searching for something, they kindly point out the truth. That which was never lost can never be found. It can never be found because it was never lost. All that really happens is that we discover that our belief that it was lost was incorrect.

Desire, then, is a key component of belief. Most of what we desire is what we want to believe – or what we don't want to believe. The impulse of desire can be very strong, so it follows that what we believe can be very strong. Just because our desires and our beliefs are strong does not mean they relate to anything truthful. Mostly the opposite is true.

We believe that what we desire will make us happy but who has ever found this to be true? When we attain what we desire, we find that we are already looking for something else. We seem not to notice that finding what we desired did not make us happy, but only led to more searching. What we are searching for is not lost.

In trying to attain what we desire, we mistakenly conclude that it must be related to pleasure. This is simply because pleasure is desirable and pain is not. This knowledge comes from the way our bodies experience the world. When we need food or water, our bodies use various physical sensations to inform us of this fact so that we may begin the process of finding food or water. Having found it the sensations in our body change and we no longer need to continue eating or drinking. Sometimes we find that once this process has begun it cannot be stopped, and so we continue eating or drinking – even though from the body's point of view it is no longer necessary.

The same process can occur with money; needing money to buy food, we begin to hoard more and more money so we can buy more and more food, even to a point where we have so much money, we could never run out of food. This also happens with sex. Having sex with the purpose of procreating is pleasurable, but we can easily adjust this so that having sex without procreating is just as pleasurable. We can have sex in ways that could never lead to procreation. So we mistakenly conclude that if having one object gives us pleasure, then having two or more objects must give us more pleasure. Before we know it we are addicted to pleasure, but now it is no longer connected to our search for food and water, or our need to procreate.

Now we search for pleasure for no other reason than that we believe it makes us happy. What we are addicted to does not make us happy; it makes us more and more addicted and, as with all addictions, the outcome is not desirable. The reason everything starts to go wrong and we begin our journey into addiction is that somehow we have moved away from the body and its network of physical sensations towards the mind. Somehow, the body and the mind have become confused. The mind seems to think it can outsmart the body with thoughts, such as 'if one of something can make me happy, two or more of that something will make me even happier'. This is very bad maths.

Some years ago, I came across a piece of research written about by Joe Dispenza, a neurological scientist. He said that scientists had discovered that the brain has two levels of functioning. The first level is the one used by most human beings. In this level, we are able to process two thousand bits of information. This is the level of the bad maths. Two thousand bits of information is the amount of information that the ego is capable of processing not the amount of information that the brain is capable of processing. This amount turns out to be four hundred billion bits of information. This makes it clear just how bad the maths used by most of the human race is. Scientists discovered that people who had practiced meditation for many years were using four hundred billion bits of information on a regular basis. It is my guess that actually we are all using four hundred billion bits of information but are completely unaware of this and therefore are unable to produce this ability on a regular basis.

The area where it is most clear to me that we use the larger amount of processing power is in the domain of the body and its senses. Visually, we see the world in intricate detail, seeing huge amounts of variation in colour, shade, light and dark, perspective and movement. I believe it would be impossible to achieve this level of perception using only two thousand bits of information. If we group all the senses together and see that in each moment we are seeing, hearing, touching, tasting and smelling then the result of all this perceptive power is truly astonishing. As I said earlier, we seem to be unaware of this huge perceptive power that we use without thinking. This power is applied and used in all situations, with all the senses working seamlessly together.

Zen Master Bankei often referred to this power as the 'unborn Buddha mind' and in his talks would often point out all the aspects of this perceptive power as it occurred. He would say things like, 'as you listen to me talking and understanding what I am saying, you are also hearing the bird that is singing outside, and all of this with no effort'. A more modern example would be driving a car.

Once we have learned to drive a car, we are able to drive and steer, adjust the amount of petrol so as to increase or decrease our speed, be aware of all other cars around us and adjust our position accordingly, be aware of the landscape and the weather and many other things while still holding a conversation with people in the car. It seems to me that we do this so easily and without any effort that we do not notice the extraordinary nature of what we are doing.

The thinking part of us, on the other hand, seems simplistic by comparison. Although the range of our thinking is vast, the actual mechanism involved is dualistic. I believe this reduces the brain's ability to process information. Dualistic thinking tends to work in a binary way, in terms of opposites such as good or bad, beautiful or ugly, black or white, or big or small. Although dualistic thinking is convenient, it also misses a lot. As it is so much a part of the way we think, our thinking tends towards the reductive. This type of thinking explains such phenomena as racism or intolerance and the attending wars and conflict that result from them.

I believe that meditation is a practical antidote to dualistic thinking. People who meditate on a regular basis exhibit far more tolerance than those who don't. They tend to be less aggressive as a consequence and more able to co-operate for the betterment of all. They are generally happier and need less to make them happy. They have the ability to learn from everything that happens to them, regardless of whether these things are pleasurable or painful. The icing on the cake is to be able to process information at the rate of four hundred billion bits per moment. Surely all of that is desirable?

4. Tree of Light

So there I was, drowning within sight of paradise. My life did not flash before my eyes. In the space of a few moments I found I had moved from a state of extreme fear to one of profound stillness. It was as though the world had stopped. In my fear I could see nothing, now I could see everything. There are fish swimming all around me as I sink. Their form, their movement and most of all their colours entrance me. I am completely still and have no desire to move or resist.

The water is crystal clear and the suns rays are reaching down through the water and caressing the ocean floor. Coral reefs rise before me in the distance. Within the stillness I become aware of the possibility of reaching this coral and now I have the strength and the will to do so. Now I am standing on the coral and breathing again, my mouth is only just out of the water. I am looking towards the beach; it is early morning and there seems to be no one around.

Something has happened to me. I remain completely still within, there is no fear. I wait, feeling the waves gently lapping around me. There are no thoughts; there is only the observation of the world around me. When my breathing returns to normal, I slowly and gently swim back to the beach. I remember who I was before this incident but now I am someone else. Before I had been in great emotional pain and had wanted to die. In those few moments in the sea this all changed. It was not that I now wanted to live; now the question does not arise. Two weeks later I found myself in Mumbai in India. I had no money left and was in the process of being repatriated. The British Embassy arranged for me to stay somewhere and gave me some money for food while I waited for a flight back to England.

In the time since almost drowning, I felt very strange; everything felt new. I felt I was learning to live all over again. Every sight and sound felt fresh and uncontaminated by past memories.

When consciousness is fresh in this way, the world is a wonderland. I am reminded of a man who had suffered brain damage, which left him with access to only very short-term memory. Whenever his wife returned after leaving the room, he behaved as though she were returning after many years absence. He was absolutely overjoyed to see her, even though she may only have left the room for a few minutes. This was much more extreme than what I was experiencing, but something similar was occurring for me.

I had to wait about four days for my flight home. During this time, I took to walking about the area near the Gateway of India. One day I was standing in the street within sight of the Gateway. I remember looking around and seeing a number of small dramas unfolding. There was a young man sleeping on a low wall who, upon waking, found that someone had used a razor blade to cut out one of the pockets on the back of his jeans. The thief had taken his wallet with his passport and all his money. The young man ran around, asking people if anyone had seen anything. There was a young boy with no legs, propelling himself up and down the street on a wooden trolley and begging. Then a man walked past me who suddenly appeared to go crazy. This man began stripping his clothes off until he was naked. He then started running around and screaming. Almost immediately, a police van screeched to a halt and a number of policemen with sticks jumped out of the van and began beating the man. They then bundled him into the van and drove off. While all this was going on I remember not feeling very much. I felt like I was watching a movie.

In front of me there was a palm tree. I remember looking up at the tree, when all of a sudden, the tree seemed to explode into multicoloured fragments of light. The best way I can describe this is that I seemed to be seeing the molecules of which the tree was composed. These molecules were all in movement, flowing in extraordinary patterns of light and colour. I found myself crying. For the first time in my life, I was aware of the truly miraculous nature of the world we live in. This was more than just beauty; I was seeing a world filled with meaning and order, yet a meaning beyond words and an order beyond all earthly order.

After a while, the tree returned to its usual appearance but the feeling of wonder that had gone with this vision remained with me for another two weeks. Although this feeling reduced in the course of time, it has never quite left me.

Within days of this event, I was back in England. For a year, I got on with my life, but this was a different life to the one I had known before these events in India. Before going to India, there had always seemed to be a sense of chaos in my life. Now I could clearly see that the chaos was the result of the way I had been looking at the world. Looking at the world through a piece of red glass makes everything appear red. In my case, everything appeared chaotic, but it was not the world that was chaotic it was my mind that had been in a state of confusion. Now the confusion was gone.

About a year later, I went back to India with a very different purpose. Before, I had wanted to die, but now I wanted to understand what had happened to me during my first trip. Of all the events that had occurred on that first trip, it was those few moments in the ocean when even the fear of death dissolved to be replaced with absolute clarity that I most wanted to understand. I realise now that I wanted not just to understand this, but to experience it again.

I remember reading about Carl Jung almost dying on the operating table and how angry he felt at being brought back to life. Somewhere seemed more preferable to Jung than his ordinary life, but I am sure this somewhere is not a place and that he did not need to die to be there. It is like a moth drawn to a flame, even though the flame may in the end kill the moth, the moth always returns. I had to return because nothing else in life could compare with that timeless moment. Even when we don't know this, we still have to return to what we truly are.

Without any clear plans, I followed my nose and at some point ended up in a place called McCloud Ganj in Dharamsala. I stayed at the Old Palace, apparently the place where the Dalai Lama had stayed when he first came to India. It was the monsoon season and I loved it. The rain would fall very hard most mornings, but by afternoon the sun would be shining and the world would sparkle. While in McCloud Ganj I met Nigel Martin, who became a very close friend. I have very fond memories of the two of us playing our guitars in the wonderful Indian evenings.

One day, I went with Nigel and two other friends up into the mountains to a place we had discovered a few days before. My friends and I had decided to spend a few days there and we set up camp in a wonderful spot beside a mountain stream. Close by there was a series of waterfalls descending down the valley from high up in the mountains. A couple of days later back in McCloud Ganj, I met a young man from Ireland in a café and found myself telling him about this place I had been to beside the waterfalls. He was one of those people that I found I had an immediate connection to; like meeting an old friend. We drank tea and talked for about an hour, after this I never saw him again.

A short time later, I met a German girl who told me about a meditation retreat she was planning to attend. She told me it was a Vipassana retreat led by an English man who had become a Theravadan monk in Thailand. He was running retreats in various places around India including Dalhousie and Goa. The next retreat in a few days time was in Dalhousie, a beautiful hill station that had been popular with the British in the days of the Raj.

I have often felt that there are people who come into my life and seem to be there for only a short time, yet are there to point out some particular information or to set me off in a new direction. I think of these people as guides who may or may not be aware of what they are pointing out to me. This was one of those times and the German girl was one of those people. I immediately decided to go, even though I was told that the retreat was fully booked. I never doubted for a moment that somehow I would find a way to attend.

I travelled with the German girl part of the way on a bus and the rest of the way on a truck. In the back of the truck was a man with a pig. The pig spent most of the trip defecating, which was not surprising as the pig was to be butchered at our destination. We did not know this at the time. We found out while walking around in Dalhousie and meeting the man who had owned the pig. He had part of the pig's carcass slung over his back, which he pointed to as he passed with a big grin on his face.

The retreat was being held in a big Victorian house high up above Dalhousie on a mountainside that overlooked the foothills of the

Himalayas. On arriving at the house I went to see the monk who was running the retreat to ask if I could attend. He confirmed what I had been told; that the retreat was fully booked. I told him that I was determined to attend the retreat and asked him again if there was any way this could be arranged. He thought about it for a while, then told me to leave it with him and he would see what he could do. Later, he told me that I could attend the retreat but that I would have to stay in another house a short walk away from where the retreat was being held.

The house turned out to be a lovely little cottage owned by an old Indian woman who could speak only a little English. The view from this cottage was one of the most beautiful I have ever seen. Close by, there was a chai shop perched on the side of the mountain where you could drink delicious chai and eat the most amazing Indian savouries and sweets while looking out towards the Himalayas. The view was truly awe-inspiring; there was a sense of vastness here that I never tired of experiencing.

Each morning during the retreat I would wake up, wash and then be served with porridge by the Indian lady. It became a ritual for me to follow the road outside the cottage right around the mountaintop, which took about half an hour and had the most spectacular views. There was a place on this walk where I would often stop and which seemed almost too perfect to be true. It was a small wood, the ground of which was completely covered in the most beautiful shades of green moss. Everywhere I looked I saw tiny streams, and dotted all over the moss were mushrooms of every shade and colour. Shafts of sunlight sliced through the canopy of trees and all was well with the world.

During another walk around the mountain, I came across a group of silver-haired monkeys. The adults were quite large but there were also many infants.

I could see them ahead of me, across the road I was on. To get past them, I had to turn back or go through them. It would probably have been wiser to go back the way I had come, but I decided to go through them. As I walked through, all the monkeys stopped and stared at me. I walked very slowly and tried to keep away from the infants and eventually made it through.

I thought at the time, and still do to this day, that this ritual walk and the experiences I had on it were an essential preparation for the meditation that was to follow. The retreat began and it was tough, but it was exactly what I wanted. The retreat was to last ten days.

In the first few days, we learnt to scan the body, working from the top of our heads to the tips of our toes. This was done very slowly, taking time to experience every sensation in the body. Each meditation session lasted an hour and was done cross-legged on the floor. Every day was filled with many hours of meditation, from early in the morning until late in the evening. We were told not to read or talk or even look out of the windows at the spectacular views. I found sitting cross-legged for an hour at a time to be very painful.

After this, we learnt the *vipassana* form of meditation, which is basically to be aware of our in-breath and out-breath by focusing on the sensation of coolness where the breath enters and leaves the nostrils.

Throughout each day, we would alternate sitting meditation, standing meditation and walking meditation. Even though this retreat was very difficult and painful for me, I felt totally committed and there was nowhere in the world I would rather have been. Every hour opened up new vistas of my inner world. From the beginning, I felt a need to be compassionate with myself and to not push too hard. To this end, I would take breaks that I thought of as longer walking meditation. I was aware that in doing this I was breaking the rules. On these breaks, I would get away from the house and walk slowly on the circular road around the mountaintop. I would usually stop at the chai stall for chai and something called milk cake that was completely addictive.

One day, as I completed my circuit round the mountaintop and was approaching the chai stall, I saw the English monk and some of his friends sitting at the chai stall. We all laughed. It seems I was not the only one that chose to be compassionate with himself.

Throughout Buddhist literature, there are stories telling of the enormous struggles men and women have made to attain enlightenment. The story of the Buddha is a good example of this. The Buddha struggled so hard that he almost killed himself. On the verge of death, he was found by a young girl who nursed him back to health; someone who showed more compassion for him than he could find for himself. From this point on, he began to find his middle way and at the same time saw the need for more compassion.

There are further strikingly similar examples of this in the lives of Zen master Bankei and Jesus. The problem seems to be in the idea that great effort involves great hardship or pain. I believe this is not the case, especially when it comes to meditation. A healthy respect for our mind and our body along with a steady persistence is all that is required. The very idea of enlightenment also poses a huge problem, because in this idea is our final conflict with ourselves. 'Enlightenment' implies a state superior to the one we are presently in. Enlightenment, therefore, implies the struggle to be something we are not and this must involve conflict, which in turn stops us from ever achieving this imaginary goal.

In the last meditation session of the last day of the retreat, something extraordinary happened. As I sat down on the floor preparing to begin the meditation, I felt something shift in my consciousness. I suddenly felt more focused than I ever had in my life.

As I began to meditate, I found I was able to stay totally focused as I followed my in-breath and out-breath. In a very short space of time, I began to experience a profound stillness and a feeling of my mind literally expanding to fill the meditation hall. I became aware of a presence residing in that stillness. This presence was full of intelligence, but completely devoid of movement or meaning. There was a huge sense of intelligent awareness that simply was. This did not feel like something personal to me, but rather something that included me and everything else.

During this meditation period, I experienced no pain – even though every meditation session prior to this one had been intensely painful. Afterwards I realised that this experience was somehow connected to my near-death experience in Sri Lanka and the tree of light experience in Mumbai.

The next morning, I walked down to Dalhousie. The stillness was still with me as I entered the town for the first time in ten days. I felt like I was descending into a beautiful world of chaos. I was reminded of the day in Mumbai when I had observed all the little dramas going on around me. As I walked through the town I realised that I had a choice. I could choose to stay up on the mountaintop, here or somewhere else, or I could choose to stay in the chaos. I realised that England was the chaos I knew something about, and it made sense to me to go back there. Before going home, I decided to continue on my travels to South East Asia, Thailand, Malaysia and then on to Australia. After working for three months in Australia, I decided to go back to England.

Within a short time of getting back, I received a letter from Nigel

Martin who told me that after I had left McCloud Ganj, the Irish man I had talked to had gone missing. Nigel said that search parties were out scouring the area for him. A few weeks later, I received another letter from Nigel telling me that the Irish man had been found at the spot I had told him about. It seems he had somehow fallen over one of the waterfalls and probably died of exposure. His body had been partly eaten by animals.

This was a terrible lesson on cause and effect for me. I realised that the Irish man had gone to this spot in the mountains and died as a direct consequence of what I had told him. I knew that what I had said to him was entirely innocent but it had been a factor leading to his death. Since that time, I have felt a great sense of responsibility for my words and actions. Who knows what effect our words and actions may have on others – and indeed what effect the words and actions of others may have on us? We live in a world of infinite possibilities; all things affect all other things.

Sometimes, we can perceive part of what we have created as in my example above. More often we never see the results of our words and actions.

The best way I can describe my experience of the years following my experience in Sri Lanka is that I seemed to be in a prolonged state of passive observation. I was seeing the world anew, with a much greater capacity to see the world as it is than ever before. I became aware that this was a process. Much of the time, I was seeing the world afresh. After a while I would drift back to seeing the world in the old way. The discrepancy between these two ways of seeing was quite shocking; after drifting into the old way of seeing, I was much more aware of how unhelpful or inappropriate this was.

A more concrete way of describing this process occurred many years later when I began work in a psychiatric unit. I began work in this unit without any real experience of working with children or of understanding what was meant by the term 'mental illness'. Because of the process I had experienced, I instinctively understood how to approach this 'problem', which is basically the problem of not knowing.

The problem of not knowing is also the solution. By allowing myself to remain in a state of not knowing, a paradox occurs in which a new kind of knowing begins to appear.

This phenomenon often occurs in my psychotherapy practice. If I just relax and don't even try to know what is going on with a particular client, this new kind of knowing takes place and happens without the least trace of effort. It has taken many years to learn to trust this state of not knowing, especially in psychotherapy, where it is very hard to let go of the idea of trying to 'fix' someone.

In the psychiatric unit, after staying in this state of unknowing for about six months, this new kind of knowing began to percolate through. Suddenly I began to act. This was not action as a result of thinking; rather it was action as a result of seeing and as such was completely spontaneous. I suddenly found my voice. That six months of observation began to pay dividends in that I could often see the bigger picture of why children or adults behave in the way they do.
For the next eight years, I became a very active part of a team working with children who displayed many different examples of so-called mental illness. I say 'so-called', because I came to see that this term is very misleading. Once we think about this as 'mental illness' we become unable to see the truth of what we are actually witnessing.

5. Everything That is Not a Belief is True

The White Queen: *'Why, sometimes I've believed as many as six impossible things before breakfast.'*

Lewis Carrol, *Through the Looking Glass*

Where there is a problem, there is sure to be a belief not far away. All wars and all conflicts are always about beliefs. What exactly is belief? Without thought, there can be no belief. The first question we need to ask in order to understand the nature of belief is, what is thought? A thought can never be anything real; a thought can only ever be an abstraction that is a mental symbol of something we consider real.

The word 'cat' is used to communicate to each other or to ourselves the idea of a creature with certain attributes that we can conveniently refer to as a cat. It seems obvious that this word actually has nothing to do with any creature at all. It allows us to communicate and this can be useful, but this word has nothing to do with any actual creature. The word 'cat' is an abstract replacement or symbol for something that cannot be known and that in the end can only be referred to as a mystery. This is true for all other words that refer to things. All things are impossible to identify at all, which is why it is convenient to pretend that we can. Words and language have no meaning – except the meaning we give to them.

Have you ever noticed how easy it is to say something to someone and realise that what you have said is not what the other person heard? For a psychotherapist, this is a very common experience. Why is this? Generally, if you understand a particular language, there should be no discrepancies. However, this is not the case because it is not just language we are talking about, it is human experience. It is our own particular human experience that colours and distorts the words and language we use, so that what we say may be in English but is only intelligible to ourselves.

It is not possible for any word to convey the mystery that is at the heart of all things, and at the heart of existence itself.

We are not good with mystery; we much prefer to know things, even when those things we know are not true and even when those things cause us extreme pain. Knowing is considered to be one of the most positive attributes of the human race, and how much you know is a yardstick to measure what you are worth. This is all back to front. In Zen Buddhism, for instance, the state of not knowing is considered to be wisdom or enlightenment. Not knowing is not a state of stupidity, it is the recognition that we know what we know, only because we believe we know it. The thing we like least of all is nothing, or space. Even these words become strangely known by the very act of turning them into concepts.

For many, it is almost impossible to be truly silent because our world is a world of sound and fury. If there is no sound we can anchor to, we create our own internal sound-scape of thinking. Often we cannot sleep because this sound-scape has taken over and we are unable, or perhaps unwilling, to switch it off. In true silence you or me no longer exists and wrongly we equate this with death. In some sense this is true; it does seem that if we do not exist then we must be dead. As with all things we believe to be true, this is not the case – unless we believe it to be true. In true silence, we are more alive than can be imagined, but because we fear this supposed state of non-existence we can never find this out. True silence is not about the absence of sound but the absence of thought. This can only be arrived at when thought is seen for what it is. Thought is not something to be gotten rid of or forcibly stopped; it is something to be seen for what it is once and for all. When thought is truly seen for what it is, it begins to dissolve. Thought can still exist and still have a function, but it will no longer be running the show. When thought is practical and useful, it does not matter that it actually does not mean anything because it is a tool and can be used as a tool as and when it is necessary.

'Everything that is not a belief is true' is, in effect, the same as saying that what is true can never be contained in any belief, and that to hold any belief somehow removes truth or 'that which is' from our experience. When we look at the world we see only ourselves. It is not possible for that which is seen to be any different from that which sees. In the world of beliefs and concepts, and especially in the world of separation, this last statement can only be seen as nonsense. Believing that 'me' exists leads us to believe that others exist and that everything that exists is separate. Seeing that there is in fact no 'me' is the same as seeing after being blind. The truth is then revealed in all its wonder and glory and not a thing can be said of this. What others take to be reality is instantly seen to be illusion.

People tell me all the time that they are depressed or that they are angry or afraid, that they love or they hate, or are indifferent. All of these things can be seen to be illusion. It is like dreaming while being wide-awake. Every time we repeat one of these beliefs to ourselves, that belief gets stronger and is taken to be more real. Eventually, these beliefs will drive us mad, or rather these beliefs make us mad but to varying degrees according to the degree of rigidity with which the belief is held. Once we believe something to be true, a cascade of events begins that strangely seems to confirm that what we believe is in fact true.

Quantum theory seems to refer to this. What we believe appears to be infectious. Other people can be infected by what we believe to be true and, even more strangely, it seems that physical reality can be 'infected' by our beliefs. It has been observed that those faced with serious physical illness are much more likely to survive longer if they have a strong belief that they can and will survive longer. Those who do not have this strong belief seem to give up and believe whatever they are told, for instance that they will die.

As I said earlier, truth is that which is, not that which we believe it to be. We live not in the world as it is but in the world as we believe or want it to be. This can only lead to suffering. Strangely, it is often because we do not *want* to suffer that we create the very beliefs that cause us the *most* suffering. An alcoholic does not want to suffer and drinks in order to avoid suffering, but this in turn leads to more suffering. Someone who is depressed does not want to be depressed, yet this person is invariably someone whose every belief creates exactly that which they do not want. Someone who is afraid believes absolutely in that which they are afraid of and without this belief there could be no fear.

My sons often ask me about fear in relation to horror films. I always tell them that they can only be afraid if they believe something that is not true. What is it that is seen in a horror film that is not true? The simple answer is, everything. The only reasonable thing that can be said to be true about a horror film is that light is projected onto a screen. What that light means is interpreted by us in terms of belief, such as belief in monsters, but in this instance there really are no monsters – only light falling on a screen. Like thought, the light on the cinema screen can have no meaning unless we give it meaning.

We give things (light or thought) meaning because we are conditioned from birth to see these things in certain cultural, historical and human ways. I say 'human' because I assume that a dog or bird or an insect or any other species does not see things in the way we do. This human or anthropomorphic view is unique to us and is based on our physical and mental capabilities. What we see is also influenced by our sex, our culture and by the unique characteristics of our bodies. When you look at another person what do you see? All of these aspects determine what we see and what we value. These are very human values, but values cannot be taken to be true just because we have them.

Even within various human cultures, these values and ways of seeing things can vary considerably. There is a tribe called the Peraha in the Amazon rainforest who see things and have very different values than people from most other parts of the world. For instance, they seem not to value knowledge that is not their own, even when that knowledge would benefit them. They refuse to build boats using knowledge from outside their tribe. Even though they were shown how to use this knowledge and build these boats, they refused thereafter to do so. When asked why they would not build these boats that were needed for fishing and hunting, they said, 'we do not build boats'.

What does the word 'believe' mean? In etymology, the root meaning is 'to make palatable to oneself, accept and approve'. This has a very broad meaning. Something is believed because, in some way, it conforms to this condition which is palatable to me. What are the conditions that make a belief palatable to *me*? Palatable can literally mean anything that suits me. There seems to be no necessity for truth in what I believe; it just has to be satisfactory to me. This means we can believe anything we want to, regardless of truth, so long as it is something that we want. A belief tells us nothing about reality it only tells us something of what different individuals find agreeable. It also tells us nothing of why each individual finds something agreeable in what they believe. What we find agreeable can range from murder, torture, and genocide to loving everyone as yourself and very many other possibilities in between.

A more useful definition of the word 'believe' is 'something that I do not know to be true'. We cannot know anything without suspending reality and making something agreeable to ourselves. This is not to suggest that we throw away language, science and knowledge, but only that we need to be very clear that these things are based on beliefs and can never be true. They can, however, be useful, but we need to be cautious because useful can be not so very different from palatable. This subject is very important for a number of reasons. What we do in this world seems to be based entirely on belief and these beliefs have a very wide range of possibilities.

Most of the horrors we see in the world would end if the rigid nature of our beliefs became more flexible. I watched a program about the Second World War in which Himmler was quoted as saying that it was acceptable to conduct medical experiments on children if it meant that German soldiers would benefit from these experiments. He also said much the same thing about thousands of Russian women dying as a result of exhaustion from digging tank traps. Apart from these horrors, Himmler was also largely responsible for the Gestapo, concentration camps and the Holocaust. This type of thinking is rigid and insane. It seems the more rigid a belief is, the more it approaches insanity. The reverse is also true. The more flexible our beliefs are, and when not taken so seriously, we begin to approach sanity. When we are not so serious about our beliefs, we become more relaxed. I am sure we have all experienced what it is like to be around someone who holds onto rigid beliefs. It is not pleasant but it is even worse for the person who holds these rigid beliefs even if they do not realise it.

This question of belief is something that the human race has to solve as we are potentially quite capable of destroying ourselves and our planet if we do not.

There is another reason why this question of belief is so important. What happens when and if our beliefs collapse? It is very difficult to put this into words, because all words are beliefs. All consciousness is also only what is believed and seeing this is only possible when beliefs collapse. It seems to me, the human race is an experiment, in what happens when we are given the power to believe, and this power is what makes us different from any other form of life on earth. This power can destroy us or free us but the freedom can only occur with the collapse of belief. It seems there is a mechanism within belief that causes its own collapse. This tends to be a slow process because it is evolutionary and occurs over millennia.

The mechanism is very simple: false beliefs inevitably lead to suffering. Also, the more rigid and false the belief, the more inevitable and extreme the suffering will be. The more we suffer, the more we are drawn towards questioning these beliefs. This does not always happen and sometimes we live, die and suffer with our beliefs intact – but this is because this an evolutionary process. This does not mean it will take thousands of years to occur, because time is another belief and it is this belief that makes the process evolutionary. At the point where we are able and willing to question our own beliefs, the evolutionary process of learning through the experience of suffering becomes redundant. To seriously question our own beliefs is the first sign of the coming redundancy of belief. When we are able to question not just what we believe but belief itself, there is no turning back. Now the process continues without effort until all beliefs are seen for what they are.

It is easy to say to someone that belief is always false and always leads to suffering, but is this understandable? In fact, this turns out to be the root of the problem. We want to understand, but understanding requires belief – so this route is impossible and futile. It is not possible to reason our way to this and there is nothing we can do to speed up the process. This does not mean we will stop trying, but this will always result in failure. Nevertheless, it is possible that one day we just stop making an effort to understand. The effort to understand results in all kinds of techniques, which we believe will improve or awaken us such as meditation. For me, meditation is 'allowing ourselves to be what we are' but even this causes a problem in that the word 'allowing' indicates effort, however subtle that effort may be, and effort is another word for trying. We will continue this endeavor until it is seen to be unnecessary.

What we are is what we always have been and always will be and nothing we can think or do can affect this in any way. One day, a creature in the ocean suddenly came out onto land and adapted to those new conditions. It is not possible to say why this happened but, it is very likely that it did.

6. The Virus

The 'I' or 'ego' is in the grip of a virus and this virus has many forms. The simplest, most universal form of the virus is pain. The purpose of the virus is to destroy all that is not true. Pain always points at and sometimes reveals that which is not true. Reality is what it is; neither good nor bad, nor anything else you could think of. What we call pain is reality and it is also neither good nor bad. We experience pain in the way we do because we believe something that is not true. You could say that when a child touches something that is hot without knowing that it is hot the virus has begun. The child does this in all innocence. This could be called a false belief because not knowing something is in a very subtle sense an assumption which is untrue. The same principle applies to any mental pain we may experience.

A child expects their mother to love him or her unconditionally but may find that this is not the case. The child experiences this as pain and comes to see that mother sometimes does not show the love that is expected but usually does. As this pattern is repeated, the child usually comes to doubt not so much their mother's ability to love, but the child's own ability to be lovable. Here again pain comes into being as a result of something believed that is not true.

We can believe something that is not true for many years – all our lives, even – but sometimes we begin to see that what we believed to be true was not. It is at this point that the virus begins to work, because seeing that what was believed to be true was in fact not true causes the pain to disappear. For the pain to completely disappear it is necessary to see completely that what we believed to be true was absolutely not true. None of this changes very much when we become adults. The adult still usually believes that if someone appears not to love them, it must be because they are unlovable.

This same reasoning can be applied to many other adult concerns such as money, power, and religion. Anytime we experience something negative, there is a tendency to relate the cause back to our sense of feeling unlovable. There are many situations in life where we come to believe, and are coerced by society into believing, that we are not good enough or that we are unlovable. These beliefs about our worth always cause pain because they are untrue. When these beliefs are seen to be untrue, the pain diminishes and then disappears. If at any time you experience pain in any form, ask yourself honestly and don't stop asking until you find the answer 'what is it I believe that is not true'. There is always an answer to this question, although the answer is more like a sudden realisation than any particular thought.

It may be misleading to isolate pain as being a separate factor that behaves like a virus. It may be more truthful to say that the universe, or all that exists, contains within it the absolute truth and at the same time appears to contain so much that seems not to be true. This reminds me of something Stephen Hawking said regarding the early state of the universe. He said that soon after the Big Bang, the universe was composed of matter and anti-matter and that as these two cannot exist in the same space they began to destroy each other. It so happened that the amount of matter in the universe was greater than the amount of anti-matter. What was left after this process of destruction was the excess percentage of matter that the universe had contained at the beginning. This excess matter now forms the universe as it is today.

This same process could be said to be taking place right now in consciousness. What arises in consciousness is all that is not true – or anti-matter. In this case, when that which is untrue meets that which is true, the survivor of this meeting is truth. The question then is, what exactly is it that is untrue? The biggest clue we have of this is pain. I see that throughout my life the pain I have experienced always existed as a result of believing something that was not true. For a number of years now, the way I have experienced pain has changed. It is not that I no longer experience pain, but rather that I no longer believe something that is untrue that gives pain its power. I am referring to the more obvious aspects of pain, such as physical pain and the mental aspects of pain that tend to arise as a result of feeling unlovable. This pain arises when we feel angry or rejected or almost any negative feeling we may have.

Beyond these layers, there are other deeper layers that are more to do with the fact of existence. By this, I mean the beliefs required to maintain the illusion that we exist as a separate identity. These beliefs are untrue. Because they are untrue, there is a need to become something more than we perceive ourselves to be. This belief can be seen in all people throughout the world, regardless of race, culture, or religious beliefs. Religious or spiritual beliefs are the more obvious aspects of our desire to be more than we are. As long as we desire to be more than we are, we must experience pain – but not the kind of pain I mentioned earlier. This pain is much more subtle and manifests as a constant movement away from what we are.

What we are can never be truly known and this is intolerable to us, because if what we are is truly unknowable, we believe it would mean that we do not exist and not existing is deeply embedded in consciousness as death. Here again we find ourselves trapped in a world of thoughts and beliefs that are not true, so this conclusion of not existing and death are also not true. Once we begin to suspect that these thoughts and beliefs cannot be true, the whole framework of consciousness begins to collapse. It is no longer necessary to believe anything. What we call 'consciousness' is nothing more than thought or belief. These thoughts and or beliefs range from the very obvious, like 'I like oranges and dislike apples' to the incomprehensibly subtle. To see a tree and recognise it to be a tree occurs whether we are thinking about the tree or not; this is what I mean by 'the incomprehensibly subtle'. Without these thoughts or beliefs, we could not even know that there is such a thing as a tree or even that the universe or 'I' exist. Thought and beliefs are essentially untrue; as consciousness itself is composed of these, all that we experience in consciousness is untrue.

You might say that if someone punches you, it is experienced to be true, but even so the whole of that experience arises in consciousness which itself is no more than a very subtle and complex bundle of thoughts and beliefs. This consciousness is made up of all that you see and experience in the world. Believing that 'I' exist, it becomes imperative to prop up something that does not in fact exist at all, with a never ending supply of more and more thoughts and beliefs. This 'I' needs feeding and is extremely hungry; without food, it will cease to exist. The most popular food seems to be anything we desire. Religious or spiritual beliefs are also very popular forms of nourishment. Throughout history, a huge market has grown out of this religious or spiritual need. There has always been and probably always will be this market where there is always someone willing to sell you what you desire. This could be God, heaven, or eternal life. Perhaps more often these days it is how to be successful and wealthy and get all that you desire.

How many times have you heard the words in advertising 'because you are worth it'? In the spiritual sense there are endless gurus and teachers who will sell precisely what you want; a world of love and beauty and preferably enlightenment. The desire for these things is food for the thought and belief systems you are composed of. These gurus and teachers are often very sincere and believe what they are saying, but again there is that word 'believe', which cannot be true. What this market is selling is the idea that there is something wrong with you. The only reason you might buy this idea is because it is the single most popular belief in the world.

There is nothing we can do, or should do, to be more than we are; the more we try, the further we move away from the unknowable truth. You are as you are and there is nothing more to be done about this. Family and society may convince you that there is something wrong with you. Of course, family and society may also have experienced being convinced by others that there was something wrong with them. Because they never questioned this, they are impelled to do the same to you. The buck can stop here if you are you willing to question this lie and free yourself of all unnecessary beliefs and so be in a position to not pass this terrible lie onto your children. I have come to see that even though I have understood for some time that all beliefs are false, I have secretly decided that some beliefs are exempt. It is these exempt beliefs that have kept the lie alive. No belief is exempt from this process.

It seems that these secret exempt beliefs are the most powerful and are those that all other beliefs rest upon. They are the beliefs that are assumed to be beyond question. Everything must go; there is no room here for secret exempt beliefs. So what are your secret exempt beliefs? This is the virus; once started, it cannot be nor should it be stopped. When the virus has finished its work this psychosis that has infected us all will be over.

My secret exempt beliefs included the belief that I exist; this is the root of all beliefs and will be preserved as long as is possible even if intellectually it is understood that this cannot be. The other more particular secret exempt beliefs were to do with certain experiences I have held and written about, like my drowning experience and certain experiences in meditation. I realise now that I have no way of knowing the nature or meaning of these experiences without invoking beliefs of some kind. Seeing this, I see that no one else has this ability either – to know the nature or meaning of his or her experiences. Therefore, 'I' have nothing to teach and nor does anyone else.

7. Truth is Devoid of all Qualities

The ego is the source of all fear. It lives in fear and the denial of truth. We could say that the ego is afraid of dying, but this would not be accurate because it does not exist in the first place. When we are still, mentally and physically, we are no longer reinforcing the illusion that we exist as a particular identity. The ego is only concerned with that which is false; that which is true is infinitely threatening. In the world, that which is false is usually held in the highest esteem.

Our purpose in life is to clearly identify what is true and what is false. Why would we prefer the false to the true? It can only be because we feel we gain something by accepting the false. At the same time, we must feel that we will lose something if we accept the truth. So what could it be that we feel we will gain or lose? Most of our behaviour is determined by our relationship to power, so it is likely that what we gain or lose in terms of the true or the false has something to do with power. The false becomes desirable if it allows us to maintain or increase our sense of power. It is not necessary to actually be powerful – it is only necessary that we *feel* powerful. Of course, the only reason we would wish to be powerful is because we do not feel powerful. Dictators, bullies, criminals and many others take power, not because they are strong, but because they feel inadequate or weak. If they did not feel inadequate or weak, they would have no need to take power from anyone.

It is surprisingly easy to feel powerful. Truth, logic, or even sanity is not required. Think of a bully; of how easy it is for the bully to feel powerful. The bully feels inadequate and so looks around for someone he or she perceives to be more inadequate or weaker than him or herself. It is only necessary for the bully to find a victim. He or she is not concerned with truth or logic and it is not even necessary to act in any physical way to attain power. The easiest possible way to attain power is through thinking. The thought 'you are stupid' is powerful because internally we have adjusted the balance of power in our favour, even though the other person may not know about it. Truth is devoid of qualities; everything that has qualities is not the truth. When we do not impose qualities or values upon the world, truth becomes a naturally occurring movement in our lives. Sanity or insanity is determined by the degree to which we believe our own thoughts. In this sense 'I love you' or 'I hate you' are exactly the same; they are both thoughts, and thought is thought regardless of the particular meanings we may invest in it. Prior to thought, there is physical sensation and it is in this area that the dominance of thinking can be dissolved. Sanity is when the physical sensations we experience prior to thought are allowed to come and go without adding any meaning. I realise that what I have just said seems almost impossible to achieve. It requires that we live in the world without imposing meaning on it. What we find when we stop imposing meaning on the world is that what is left is physical sensation and this has no meaning. Physical sensation does, however, have a purpose.

The purpose of physical sensation is in the way it enables us to perceive and interact with the world. Physical sensation is deeply connected to consciousness and without it we could not be conscious. We give these physical sensations meaning in a misguided attempt to control them. By giving physical sensations meaning, we set in motion something that becomes a much greater problem than the original problem. 'Control' is another word for repression; something that we do not like is repressed. Repression is similar to sweeping dirt under the carpet; we cannot see it but it is still there and, in the case of repression, continues to cause negative effects. It is useful to think of physical sensation as truth that just is, regardless of what we think.

It is difficult to understand the idea that truth is devoid of qualities. How can we describe, relate to, or think about something that has no qualities? This seems to me to be at the heart of our problem. The possibility that there may be something devoid of qualities and further that this something is who we really are is like trying to catch air with a butterfly net. We know that a group of people observing a crime often report wildly different versions of what happened.

We also know that the way two different people deal with the same situation can be very different; even the emotions they may have may be very different. This must be to do with the particular meaning that each of us gives to the world. The range of meanings at our disposal seems endless.

Without access to the part of us that is devoid of qualities, we tend to move further and further away from what is true or further away from what works. As with most things in life, what is needed is a balance. In this case the balance is between what is devoid of qualities and meaning and that which of necessity must be given qualities and meaning. It is much easier to talk about qualities and meaning than to talk about that which does not have qualities or meaning, but I will try. That which is without qualities or meaning is always present. In whatever you are doing or experiencing right now, it is present. There is no time when this is not present and there is no time when it has ever changed to any degree whatsoever. You are what you have always been; it is just that superimposed over this is a projection of the particular bundle of meanings you have accumulated in your life. When we look at someone, we are mostly looking at a predetermined idea of what or who we are looking at. This predetermined idea is based on all our prior experiences and is calculated and formed in the blink of an eye. Once the idea has formed, we are trapped; we become convinced by our own belief about what we are looking at and this is taken as reality. Even while we are doing this, the truth is still available if we could only turn our attention in the right direction. The right direction is not outwards onto the object of our attention, but inward to the source of our attention itself.

In the space between thought is that which we truly are. As we abide in that space, the world of belief and meaning are revealed for what they really are. They are revealed to be illusory; to have no existence. In this, all the false beliefs of the world are easily and effortlessly seen.

8. Self-Enquiry

If we can eliminate all the parts of us that are subject to change, what remains is that which is not subject to change. Ramana Maharshi and others referred to this process as self-enquiry. Self-enquiry is the act of seeing what we really are. What is most helpful in this process is finding our way to the truth that we are not the body, nor are we the mind, because both of these are subject to change. With a gentle persistence, we notice that anything that arises that is subject to change has nothing to do with who or what we truly are. At this point, happiness, unhappiness, pain or pleasure or my mind assigning any meaning to anything, become helpful aspects of this process. The reason these objects of change become helpful is because, once we start to pay attention to this aspect of reality, we notice that actually that which is changeable is really quite obvious. As any of these objects of change arise, notice that what arises is subject to change and is therefore not related to who I really am. The problems of my life arise when I assign meaning to reality.

Reality occurs in the moment prior to meaning. Do not make a problem out of something that arises; just see the truth of exactly what it is that arises. If I ask you to focus your attention on any object right now, I assume you can do it. If I then ask you to focus your attention on another object, the same applies. I am just pointing out a simple truth that you have the power to focus your attention on anything you wish. If I ask you to focus your attention on who or what you really are, that should not be a problem, but somehow that becomes the ultimate problem. Why is this? Simply because who we think we are is not who we really are, so when asked to focus your attention on who you really are, you find yourself focusing your attention on who you really are not. Asking 'what' we really are rather than 'who' we really are is another step in the right direction.

In Zen Buddhism, a method was developed that was designed to help with this problem. The method required working with a 'koan'. A koan is a problem that cannot be solved using the intellect or the ego. What do you do if you are given instructions to solve a particular problem without recourse to your intellect or ego? What you invariably do is carry on trying to solve the problem with your intellect or ego. Even if you were told that it is impossible to solve this problem with your ego, you would continue trying. Why is this? It is because for most of us our attention is fixed firmly on the part of ourselves that is not real. This part of ourselves that is not real becomes *so* real that we cannot even imagine there could be any other part involved in who we are. Throughout the ages, there have been those who solved this dilemma and found who they really are. When Buddha became enlightened, it is said that he originally believed that it would be impossible to communicate his understanding or experience to others. It is not impossible but it is so subtle that we invariably overlook what is right there before us.

Who you really are shines out from within all the things that you are not. It is always there; it is not subject to change. There is no time when it is not there, even when your mind is focused on what you are not. The process of self-enquiry requires us to turn our attention inward, to that subtle sense of self that tells you only that you exist. It does not tell you what it is that exists only that something exists. As you attempt to do this, all the things that you are not will begin to arise. As you notice these things, such as thoughts, feelings or images, be aware that all of these are clearly subject to change and are therefore not what you really are. This process will only be available to you when you are ready. If you are not ready, it will all sound like madness.

This process does not require that you understand it, but rather that it resonates with you in such a way that there is a kind of faith or trust in the idea. Likewise, turning your attention inwards to that subtle sense of self that tells you only that something exists requires a kind of faith or trust – or else why would you do it? In the beginning, all this obviously requires effort. Eventually, effort falls away and the process continues much like stepping off a cliff. Once you have made the effort to step off the cliff, nothing more needs to be done – except maybe to scream or just experience the sense of flying!

9. A Tendency to Exist

'Things have a tendency to exist'. I remember coming across this statement many years ago and sensing the truthfulness of it. Now I am more certain of its truthfulness than ever. One might think this extraordinary statement was made by someone talking about magic, but it was made by a scientist talking about quantum physics. One could also make variations on this statement such as, 'the universe has a tendency to exist', 'the world has a tendency to exist', 'others have a tendency to exist', and 'I have a tendency to exist'. This statement strongly suggests that the world is not as solid or as permanent as we might think. Mostly what we see and experience holds true, that is; it does not appear to change.

It is this quality of predictability that allows us to achieve so much. We can build extraordinary buildings because laws of science hold true. The same can be said for most areas of human endeavour, whether artistic or scientific. This is so much the case that it becomes almost impossible to imagine a situation where it would not be true. In the world of predictability, all is cause and effect; it is observable and demonstrable. If you drop a cup on a hard floor it will probably break, but it will certainly fall, and at a very predictable velocity. This is an immensely powerful aspect of the world; if we know the rules, it seems that almost anything is possible. Even in the world of art and music, this holds true. There are always rules, even if at some point we decide to break them. Even when we break the rules, we end up creating new rules; jazz and abstract art would be examples of this. In science, the rules are constantly changing. The rules that existed a thousand years ago or just yesterday no longer apply. Adhering to these rules can be unbelievably powerful in terms of great art, great music, wonderful architecture and amazing technology. Most of us would not care to give up these creations, but there is a downside to these rules. What if we begin to see the world as entirely predictable?

My conception of hell is to be trapped in a world where everything is repeated and predictable. How would you feel if you knew precisely every detail of your life to come? How would it feel if someone were to give you a typed account of the conversation you were about to have? These are extreme scenarios I am using to make my point. What if our minds become so full of these predictable rules that we become trapped and can no longer conceive of reality being any other way? Think about some of these 'rules': we are born and we will die; every day we get older and approach our end. We may have rules that say the world is painful and people are untrustworthy. We may even have rules like those of Hitler or Stalin which make it possible to commit any atrocity imaginable. Rules are infinitely creatable; if we can conceive of a rule, that rule can be turned into reality.

Sanity is not a requirement for rules; the ability to conceive and justify is the only requirement for creating rules. Hitler conceived a rule of making jews, gypsies, gay people and many other minority groups inferior to himself or to the master race. Based on this rule, he proceeded to his next rule which is that these inferior people had no rights. Ultimately, this led to the rule that these people deserved to die. His justification was that he was purifying the gene pool and that, far from being the horror that it was, the holocaust was an act of good. His justification was so convincing that most of Germany went along with these rules. This is one extreme example, but the world is filled with many other less extreme yet equally crazy examples.

A rule is a statement of predictability. Once a rule is created and believed in, what follows is almost entirely predictable. The creation of certain rules is responsible for many negative aspects of human behaviour. All human interactions are based upon certain rules. These rules tend to have little relationship to reality. The outcome of any human interaction is totally determined by the rules created by the individuals or groups involved. If we can learn to understand the rules that have been created by any individuals or groups, the possibility of an unpredictable or creative outcome becomes possible. If we can learn to understand the rules that we create for ourselves, it becomes possible to be free of these rules and to live a truly creative life. A creative life is not a predictable life. What is predictable is not creative.

Clearly, there are areas in life that require predictable rules and, equally, there are other areas that require creativity. What becomes possible when we are no longer constrained by our own rules of predictability? Throughout the ages, there have been individuals who have transcended the rules held by the majority. To some of these individuals, we give the name 'genius; and others we may call 'lunatics'. Although there are risks involved in transcending our own rules, there is an even greater risk if we do not. We can diminish the risk if we can remain flexible. If we can remain free of giving reality any fixed meaning, there is no risk whatsoever.

Things have a tendency to exist. What we believe exists *does* exist, but not before we believe it. If we believe we are depressed, then this will be true or become true. We begin to scan the world, looking for confirmation that our belief is true. Often, doctors or psychiatrists will be happy to confirm this for you and even give you more proof in the shape of certain medications. I am not saying that prescribing medication for depression is never justified, but there is a danger of confirming beyond all doubt that someone is depressed. Likewise, if we believe we are unlovable, or stupid, ugly or any other negative belief these perceptions will become true. To become true, all that is required is that we believe something. Believing we are unlovable is probably the most negative and serious belief we can hold – apart from one other which I will come to later. This may be further complicated by the fact that we are not aware that we believe we are unlovable. When we believe we are unlovable, a number of subsidiary beliefs come into being. All subsidiary beliefs have only one purpose, which is to confirm the original belief that we are unlovable. Subsidiary beliefs tend to involve limitations. For instance, the belief that the work I do is the only work I could do, even though I do not like this work I feel compelled to keep doing it. If asked, I might find some justification as to why I do this work or why it is impossible to conceive of changing it.

In a way, all addictions involve these subsidiary beliefs. In the act of drinking alcohol, there is the knowledge that this substance is harmful yet we choose to drink it anyway. We may justify this in many ways, the simplest and most effective way being 'I like drinking'. Even though this justification enables us to continue drinking something that is actually classified as poison, we are still aware on some level that we have an intention to harm ourselves. This unconscious knowledge becomes further proof of our belief that we are unlovable. Any intention to harm oneself consciously or unconsciously cannot be an act of love. If you see an animal chewing on its own leg, you would assume something must be wrong, either with the leg or with the animal.

Working in a psychiatric unit, I often saw young boys and girls purposely harming themselves. The most common method they used was to cut themselves with bits of glass. The rule here seemed to be 'if living in this world involves me experiencing pain, then it is preferable that I be the one to administer the pain'. Although there is a strange logic to this rule it is not difficult to see that the rule actually makes no sense. Surely it is bad enough when others hurt you without choosing to harm yourself.

Some years ago while attending a process-work workshop, a situation arose that gave me an insight into this mechanism. The workshop involved watching demonstrations of process-work in action and then getting into small groups and practising some of the techniques we had been shown. At one point, a young woman who was known to self-harm began banging her head on a table. This went on for a while, with no one attempting to stop her. Then the leader of the workshop came up behind her, placed his hand on her head and proceeded to bang her head on the table. The woman seemed outraged by this, but if her purpose was to harm herself why then was it so unacceptable for someone else to do the harming? It was acceptable for the woman to harm herself because she was in control of the harming. When someone took away this control, she was outraged. This is all very strange. Harming ourselves for no apparent reason is unusual. We may call it mental illness, but this is too easy; we do not do things without a reason. Even the so-called mentally ill do what they do for a reason. It is just that often we do not know what the reason is. Calling someone mentally ill solves this problem, because now we do not need to know why; we just need to assign a category to someone we do not understand, and place him or her in it. It is very strange that we can harm ourselves for no apparent reason but this does not mean there is no reason.

When we are children and we experience pain that we do not

understand and cannot control, we instinctively choose a different kind of pain that we can control. It is almost as though we are saying, 'if being alive involves feeling pain then I am going to take control of this pain. From now on, if I am to be hurt then it is I that will do the hurting'. When I see someone harming themselves in any way, I see someone taking control of their pain. This is the solution of the ego; if I am to experience pain, it is better that I be the one to inflict that pain.

The other serious negative belief we hold is probably the most difficult to understand. We believe that we exist, when in fact this is just a belief or a story we tell ourselves.

At this point, you may be thinking I have completely lost the plot. What I am asserting is not new and has been spoken of for thousands of years. In this last sentence, who is the 'I' that is asserting anything? This 'I' that I refer to is the same 'I' that you and all others refer to as the one who is saying, thinking or doing anything. What 'I' am saying and what others have said before me is that this 'I' that I believe myself to be is in fact not the 'I' that I really am. Bear with me, because our understanding of everything hinges on it.

In Buddhism, it has been asserted that the 'I' or the ego is an accretion of thoughts and ideas that have no substantial reality apart from the belief that they exist. The part of me that does exist is not subject to change; this is both a huge problem and a blessing. It is a problem because if the part of me that does exist is not subject to change it must be devoid of all qualities that are subject to change. Let us remove the qualities that are subject to change; the body is the first to go because this is the part most obviously subject to change. From the day we are born, we begin to age and whether we notice this change or not, it is happening. Next on the list is the world or the universe; clearly, this is also subject to change. In Buddhism, this is referred to as 'impermanence', a law that states that all physical objects alive or not are in the process of change. That which can change must therefore be impermanent. When you look at an object like a rock, for instance, it may appear that the rock is not changing, but we know that in time the rock will be worn down by wind and rain and eventually fall to dust. So a rock that appears not to be changing is in fact changing – but so slowly it is unobservable.

I was watching a programme on television recently in which a balloon was filled with water and then pricked with a pin. From the point of view of normal time, there is an instantaneous collapse of the balloon and the water falls in a chaotic mess. When shown slowed down hundreds of times, something else is revealed; the instant the pin pricks the balloon, the balloon disintegrates, but for a short time the water holds exactly the same shape as when the balloon was holding it.

So far, we have identified the parts that are subject to change and which are not real, such as the body and the universe. To this, we can add the mind; have you ever heard of someone changing their mind, and have you ever changed your mind? Yes, you have, more times than there are grains of sand in the Ganges (an old Buddhist joke).

So what is left after eliminating the body, the mind and the universe? Do you see now why this is such a problem? We cannot even count on the mind to look for the part that is not subject to change, because this part itself is subject to change. This can also be referred to as 'blood washing blood'; trying to wash a blood-stained garment with blood and expecting to clean it. Just because we cannot use the mind to find that part of us that is not subject to change does not mean that part does not exist. This is the blessing I referred to earlier. Let us assume that there is a part of oneself that never changes. What are the implications of that? If something is not subject to change, it is not born and cannot die.

If someone is depressed, anxious, fearful, sad or even happy, all of these are subject to change and are therefore not the truth. If I think I understand something or don't understand something, then this is also subject to change; understanding is subject to change. The body getting old, suffering illness or dying are all aspects of change. When the world or other people appear to change, something is happening that is not true. On one level, it is easy to see that things change, but to say that this is because they are untrue or illusory requires a huge leap of faith. The world is an illusion, but this is not really the problem; the problem is that we take it to be real. The illusory nature of the world is very consistent and convincing, mostly because of the way it is viewed.

What would we see if the world were slowed down like the water and the balloon? We would we see things that could not normally be seen, because the speed of our perceptions runs at a very specific rate. Much like a movie that, in order to create the illusion of natural movement, requires the film speed through the projector to run at a very specific rate. Speed up the film enough and everything becomes a blur, and all sense of detail is lost. Slow down the film sufficiently and most things appear not to move at all, but very fast objects like the balloon disintegrating suddenly reveals all their details. Apart from the speed of perception, there is also the frequency of light, the nature of the brain and the eye that determine how we see the world in a very particular way that is different from that of a dog or a cat or an insect. So which creature on this planet is seeing things as they actually are? The answer is none; each sees a version of reality that is determined by many varying factors. Again, we find we live in a world where almost nothing is as it appears and all is in the process of change. There is nothing to hold on to here, because everything is moving and unknowable, all we see are particular sounds and images that have been created in a particular way. It would be difficult to see how any two entities could be said to be seeing or experiencing the same thing at the same time.

That which is not subject to change is not really interested in the many different possibilities of perception. All perception is seen as illusory and this engenders a very different attitude to the objects of the world. Everything is seen as arising and falling away; the fact of the arising or falling away is seen but not held on to. There is nothing to hold on to. For some, this will invoke fear, but this is an error. What we should be afraid of is this ability to hold on to things like hurt, anger, sadness, jealousy and fear itself.

What is mind? Is it any more than thought? Where do thoughts come from? Mind is thought, yet there is something else that is aware that thought is happening. A computer can carry out many functions and appears to have a certain level of intelligence – in playing chess; for instance. Yet what is a computer without the mind that made it, programmed it, and is able to use and understand what the computer creates? It is nothing but plastic and metal, with no purpose and no function. Without consciousness, the universe and all it contains ceases to exist.

Something other than thought is required for comprehension to occur. This something is consciousness. Whatever is seen, heard, touched, tasted, smelled or thought about arises in consciousness. Without it, none of these qualities could arise. Although the universe and all its wonders are enthralling, consciousness is more so.

10. Home Base

'Home base' is the unconscious desire to recreate the situations, circumstances and, most importantly, feelings that dominated our early life experience. Unconscious, means that it is usually not available to our conscious mind; therefore, we have no knowledge of it. I sometimes hear people talking about their happy childhood, but they are referring to the part they are aware of – the conscious part. It is not my intention to take anyone's happy childhood memories away, but to question whether or not this childhood and the memories of it are the whole truth. Because something is not known to our conscious mind does not mean that it does not exist, or that it is not having some effect on our life. In my experience, what is held in the unconscious mind is more powerful and more active than what is held in the conscious mind. If we can identify what is held in the unconscious mind, what is identified becomes conscious. When this unconscious material becomes conscious, we begin to see clearly why we are the way we are and why we do the things we do. It then becomes possible for something to change. If this unconscious material remains unconscious and therefore unknown, it is very unlikely that anything will change.

Here are some examples. A man I know whose job is to help others build homes is at the same time trying to make his own house more homely. This man never stops trying to create a home, but his efforts are all in one direction – the physical building and furnishing of his home. Interestingly, there seems to be very little concern for someone to share that home with. Consciously, he desires a home, but his home base is not that; home base is what he is really seeking; to recreate all aspects of what was true for him as a child. There are many examples of men and women from what we call 'broken homes' that seem to always arrive back at this particular home base where the home is broken or where either they leave or are left. It is very difficult to hear this; that what we desire is not our dream of how things should be, but the reality of how it actually was.

Another example is a woman whose father left when she was young and whose mother became an alcoholic. These are the conditions for her home base; she seeks to experience again being abandoned by a man as she was abandoned by her father and to re-experience the chaos of her early life with mother. The fact that she constantly experiences life this way is not an accident. What you would expect and most people would believe is that she would desire the opposite of this home base, but there is no 'wiring' in our brain that relates to this. The 'wiring' that is there is home base or the way that the mind has become programmed.

It seems natural that we try to change that part of our life that was not happy or where we were not loved. The way the mind works, however, makes this very difficult. The mind operates according to what it knows, not according to what it does not know or to what it dreams. What the mind knows, however, it actually does not know – it only believes. Although these beliefs may be very strong, the truth is that they are false and if this is seen deeply enough, these beliefs will dissolve. Trying to be rid of our beliefs by dreaming of a world in which we are loved and are happy will not work. Instead, it is necessary to examine the nature of belief itself and discover if any belief can ever be true.

11. Perspective

A man standing at sea level can see the world from a particular perspective. If this man is able to move to a higher altitude, his perspective changes and he can see what would have been impossible to see from sea level. As this man moves higher still, he sees more and more of what previously would have been impossible to see. At a certain height, he can see that the world is round and he can see details on the surface that show a much bigger picture of the nature and organisation of the earth; of rivers, lakes, oceans, and land masses and mountain chains. Moving out further still, the earth begins to diminish and at some point looks similar to a star. Further out still and the earth disappears. What we are able to see is determined by the place we are looking from. When I was young I saw the world and myself from a particular perspective. I saw the world and myself in a more limited way. As we grow older, our perspective changes and we come to see what we could not see when we were young. It is not only growing older that changes our perspective; it is also determined by what we experience as we are growing older. It could be almost anything, but whatever we experience determines the perspective that we see from. For me, almost drowning was the single most dramatic shift of my earlier life. Suddenly, I was seeing from a very different perspective. Many of my tendencies stayed the same, but many disappeared; generally the more negative tendencies disappeared. In the years that followed, as each new perspective unfolded, I found I was pulled not so much towards new experiences but towards new perspectives. Experiences continued, of course, but slowly I began to see that in some way these were secondary to the shifts in perspective.

The greatest shift in perspective comes when we turn our attention away from the world and begin to pay attention to what it is that views the world. This is why people have practiced meditation of one kind or another for many thousands of years. The simplest and most effective form of meditation is just to remain still. To remain still is to be as we are, without any attempt to change anything. This can seem very difficult, but from a certain perspective it becomes effortlessly easy.
We come to deeply understand that absolutely no effort is required for us to be what we are. All that is initially required is that we want to know who or what we really are. Meditation is not really a technique or method although there are many variations available. All that is required is just the desire to be still and finally not even the desire to be still. We meditate because it is not understood that what we are and have always been is complete.

12. Knowing and Not Knowing

Every summer, for 12 years, I would pack my tent and go to Brockwood Park. Brockwood Park was created to give children an education that embodied the teachings of J.Krishnamurti. Every year Krishnamurti gave public talks in a marquee tent in the grounds. People were allowed to camp in these grounds for two weeks to attend the talks.

Over the years, a group began to form from the people I met here, and each year we would meet and set up our tents in the same area. In the evenings, a fire would be lit and discussions would begin. These discussions were usually about the talk that Krishnamurti had given that day. Without realising it at the time, we were doing what I have often seen Buddhist monks do – debating topics and honing the mind. Listening to Krishnamurti each day always supplied one or more topics. In recent years, Dr Joe Dispenza has stated that talking in groups and debating topics such as life, death, love, meditation, and fear causes the brain to function on a higher level.

After one particular talk, Nigel Martin and I decided to head off to Cornwall. On the way, something strange happened to me. My assumption was that something in the last talk given by Krishnamurti had triggered something in me. Nigel was driving when suddenly my mind seemed to slow down and I was able to see the inner world of my own thinking. It was like watching a television screen and seeing the credits slowly moving down the screen. Whatever was happening did not affect my functioning in any way. I was still able to communicate with Nigel and to perform any task that was required. Whenever I was free to just sit, the process would begin again. This process continued for a number of days. During this time, I was able to see the way my mind worked and see that it worked in the same way as for most other people. When I learn how to read a book, there is the potential to be able to read all books. When I am able to see and understand my own mind, there is the potential to see and understand all minds. We are all different, yet we are more alike than different. The first thing I noticed when my mind slowed down was that my mind almost never stopped moving. Even when it slowed down, there was still an almost obsessive quality to my thinking. I realised that what I thought about was not so important but it was important that I did not stop thinking.

I saw that my mind was always a few steps ahead and was continuously creating plans or strategies, even though there was nothing that really needed planning. It seemed to me that I was terrified that I might find myself without direction.

This aspect of my mind, and I believe all minds, explains why the world is in such a mess. We are driven by minds that only want to be busy. What we do in the world is therefore driven by the need to do something, rather than any consideration of what we actually do.

When our family cat died recently my younger son kept telling me all the different reasons why he thought the cat had died. From the beginning, I had told him that the cat was old and had probably died of old age. This answer did not satisfy him, so he suggested that maybe the cat died because some other children in the street had chased her recently. This would be followed by another explanation soon after. It is very difficult for us to accept that something has occurred for which we really have no explanation.

It did not matter to my son which explanation was correct; it only mattered that he could continue looking for one. Even the question of how the cat died was not the real question. The real question is, what is death? On one level, my son knew exactly what death is. It is loss and it is pain. If we are not seeking the meaning then we have no recourse but to reside in the pain. With death, this is not so difficult to see, but what about the other times – when for no apparent reason I seek to distract myself by creating plans or strategies, or by looking for meaning? If there is no pain or distraction in the present, the mind becomes aware of unresolved pain from the past. This pain seems to have no origin and is often not connected to the present. Sometimes, the pain seems to be connected to the present – when, for instance, someone insults or rejects us. It is very easy to believe that the person who has insulted or rejected us has caused us to feel pain. There is a profound principle here.

What we experience in the present is not always what it seems, because sometimes what we are experiencing is actually something from the past. Sometimes fears from the past are projected onto the present and then onto the future.

Wherever fear is projected, a neural pathway is laid down and reinforced. This continues until we are completely trapped in a world of fear.

The mind much prefers 'knowing' to 'not knowing', even when a particular knowing causes us pain and may continue to cause us pain on a regular basis. Not knowing is, I believe, deeply connected in our mind to not being, not existing, or death. It is not so much the death of the body we fear, but rather not existing as an identity. What we fear is already the case: we do not exist as an identity; we only believe that we do. This belief must actually be very fragile; in other words, maybe part of us suspects that we are not as real as we would like. There are clues to this suspicion such as preferring knowing to not knowing and the constant need to create a drama so that we may feel emotions, which in turn convinces us that we exist.

I have come to see that not knowing is never a problem. How can not knowing be a problem? It can only be a problem when there is a secret knowing.

With death, this secret is that I will no longer exist – but this turns out to be a secret knowing. How can there be a problem if we really don't know? This is the real problem right here. It is almost impossible to conceive of really not knowing, because the fear of this is stopping us from ever approaching it. This is very circular; we fear it so much that we can never approach it, and because we can never approach it we can never conceive of it. It is interesting to note here that meditation is maybe the best practice to end this stalemate. In meditation, we naturally come to see the ideas we have about ourselves begin to change and become less rigid. As these ideas become less rigid, our mind naturally becomes more flexible. We become less defensive about our beliefs and this too is very circular. As the mind becomes more flexible and less defensive, we become more able and willing to not know.

13. Paradoxical Meditation

When we meditate, we are attempting to still the mind. When we have the intention to still the mind, a paradox is created in which the mind becomes more active. The intention to meditate is the intention of the ego and the ego is the reason that the mind is not still. This is why many people find it difficult to meditate. When we try to still the mind, we are unintentionally asking the ego to get involved.

During my training as a psychotherapist, I was introduced to the work of Victor Frankl, a survivor of Nazi concentration camps, who happened to be a psychiatrist. Frankl coined the term 'logotherapy' for the style of therapy he practiced. *Logos* is the Greek word for meaning and 'logotherapy' is an existential form of therapy that deals with meaning or the lack of it in our lives. I felt a kinship with Frankl; perhaps because I had also confronted death, although not in such an extreme way. One of the techniques developed by Frankl is called 'paradoxical intention'. The moment I heard about this technique, I realised how important it was in the practice of psychotherapy. Over the years, it has become an integral part of my practice as a psychotherapist and meditation teacher.

Frankl describes paradoxical intention as a method that has the effect of 'taking the wind out of our sails'. For instance, if someone finds it difficult to sleep I might suggest that they try very hard to stay awake. When we are trying to sleep, a state of conflict or tension is created which may make it impossible to sleep. When we try to stay awake, a paradox is created that has the effect of collapsing the tension that is keeping us awake and so taking the wind from our sails.

Recently I attended a talk given by Stephen Batchelor in which he spoke about his life, which had certain parallels with my life. Stephen talked about his experiences in India in the early seventies. Stephen said that while he was in Dharamsala he had decided to become a monk. After a few years he began to feel uncomfortable with the Tibetan approach to Buddhism, in particular with their attitude to re-incarnation. He said that he felt that this belief was too rigidly held and that any questioning of it was discouraged. Stephen left Dharamsala and entered a monastery in a forest in Thailand. Here the monks practised only one meditation; to ask the question in every moment 'what is this'?

I like this meditation because it is simple and direct, and it encourages us to attend to each moment with an enquiring mind without looking for any answers to the question. Krishnamurti said much the same thing: 'full attention with a full heart in the living moment'.

During a meditation retreat I was running, an idea occurred to me regarding paradoxical intention and Zazen meditation. The practise of Zazen meditation involves sitting with the eyes open facing a wall, usually for twenty minutes. It occurred to me that these two techniques could be combined. I decided to try an experiment. I told the group what I had in mind and they all agreed to take part. I suggested to the group that the next session of meditation would be divided into two parts. In the first part, I suggested to the group that they do the opposite to what they had been doing in previous meditation sessions. I suggested that, rather than attempting to still the mind, they do the opposite and try very hard to think as much as possible. I asked them to create as much pressure as possible and not allow any gaps between thoughts. This would be done for ten minutes, after which time I would ring a bell to indicate the end of that part of the meditation and the start of the next period of meditation, in which we would return to the Zazen practice we had been doing previously. This was for a further ten minutes. This was followed by ten minutes of walking meditation, followed by a twenty-minute session of Zazen meditation. At the end of these periods of meditation, we left the meditation hall for supper. I intended to ask the group about their experiences of this experiment during supper. We were told that supper would not be ready for another twenty minutes or so. I told the group this and realised that two people were missing: Vijai and his partner Yasmine. I went back into the meditation hall and found Yasmine still sitting in her meditation position. She seemed to be alternately crying and laughing for no apparent reason, Vijai was consoling her. I waited a while and then asked Yasmine if she felt like talking about her experience. What follows is Yasmine's experience described in her own words.

For almost a week, we had been meditating – trying to empty the brain and not think of anything. Naturally, exactly the opposite happened. One afternoon, we were supposed to do exactly the opposite and think, think, think as much as we could during the first twenty minutes of the session. We started, and then the weirdest thing happened: I couldn't think of ANYTHING. I was just completely empty. I even tried to encourage myself.Come on! Think! Use this opportunity when you're at last allowed to let your thoughts run free. A bit later, I think it was when we had moved into the second part of the session (Zazen), all of a sudden my entire body felt extremely heavy. It felt as if life had departed from my body. Somehow, I knew that my body was still there, but I couldn't feel anything anymore. It was as if I wasn't inside of my own body. My breathing began to slow down to almost nothing. Then, all of a sudden, in the middle of this completely empty and somewhat weirdly balanced state, I was hit by something like lightning inside of me. A white ray moved diagonally through the front of my body, across my chest and tummy. After that an enormous heat arose from my root chakra, eventually stopping at my throat. After that, I had this deep, deep sadness arising from within that started to take my breath away. I started to cry and to sob. I was almost choking. This deep sadness interchanged several times with almost hysterical laughter, an incredibly deep sensation of relief and of 'I really don't care anymore about anything'. If anybody had asked me right there and then why I was crying or laughing, I wouldn't have been able to explain. After a while – ten or fifteen minutes, maybe it was all over. I felt tired but also extremely and deeply relaxed; somehow free. It was a huge negative energy or tension release. In the next few hours, I was aware of only one thing: 'nothing really matters'.

Over supper, the rest of the group related their experiences of the paradoxical meditation. The first thing I noticed was that there was much more energy in the group. One person said he felt angry because when he did the paradoxical meditation, he found that trying to think a lot was very difficult and he found that he could not think at all. He was angry because he realised that he likes to think. He said that he felt angry with me for taking this indulgence away from him. Most people in the group felt that their ability to meditate became easier and that their experience of meditation became deeper.

In the days that followed, the energy of the group continued to rise, with the result that I was asked to include more meditation sessions in the program. After one meditation session, Vijai said he had never experienced such stillness in his life; he had tears in his eyes as he said this. Some of the people in the group were in therapy with me, so I was able to observe firsthand some of the changes that occurred after the retreat. In one woman, I noticed an increasing ability to trust herself. I saw that she was much more confident and assertive in situations than she previously had been. After the retreat, Vijai began to experience a lot of anger, which he said was very out of character for him. Yasmine continued to experience the emotions and energy she had experienced during the retreat.

I felt that this form of meditation definitely had potential, but I felt the need to be cautious. This technique was producing dramatic results, but I needed to gain more experience of the effects it might have on people. Since the retreat, I have recommended that people only use this technique in a group setting – either in a meditation group or during a retreat. I recently ran another meditation retreat during which I began to further develop paradoxical meditation.

It occurred to me that there are two main schools of Zen: Soto Zen and Rinzai Zen. Soto Zen mostly uses Zazen as a form of meditation, while Rinzai Zen uses koan meditation. The first is considered a passive form of meditation, although there is an emphasis on applying Zazen to everyday activity such as work. There seems to be a principle at work in Zazen, in which the active grows from the passive. Koan meditation, in contrast, is much more active; a question is asked that cannot be answered by the ego. As far as I know, these two techniques have always been used separately. With paradoxical meditation I had begun to use the two types of meditation together within a session. I now considered the possibility of creating a Koan style dialogue with the ego.

During my recent retreat, I again asked the group if they were willing to try an experiment. I made it clear that people should only do this if they felt comfortable.

If they did not feel comfortable doing it, they should just carry on with the normal Zazen meditation. A few members of the group told me later that they decided not to do the paradoxical meditation. My instructions to the group were that for the first ten minutes they were to think as much as possible. The second part of the experiment I think of as 'good cop / bad cop'. This part involves the group first asking their own ego a question, in the manner of a 'bad cop'. The question to the ego was 'as you seem to think, you can always solve my problems. Tell me the solution now'. This question is asked in the form of an aggressive interrogation. It is similar to the initial paradoxical meditation, in that there is a relentless quality to this interrogation. I suggested that we should not give the ego time to answer the question. In the 'good cop' part of the interrogation, the same question continues – but this time in a softer, more gentle way. The question would now become something like 'if you know the answer to my problems, please tell me now; I really would like to know'. This part is for a further five minutes. This is followed by five minutes of Zazen meditation. At the end of this, the group sat together in a circle. I waited for people to respond to the experiment.

Within minutes, it became clear to me that something had changed dramatically within the group and there was a huge surge of energy, in marked contrast to the energy in the group prior to this experiment. People were suddenly very engaged, talking to each other and asking questions, and there was a real sense of serious enquiry in the group. There was also much laughter in the group and they seemed to me to interact in a more compassionate way. One woman in particular who had seemed to me to be depressed, suddenly did not. After talking to this woman later, she confirmed what I had perceived. She could not believe that she could have changed so much during one session of meditation.

14. The Culmination of all Karma

A client was describing something she had done that morning that she felt bad about. I asked her if she thought she could have done anything different. She replied, 'of course I could', and proceeded to tell me some of the things she could have done differently. I asked why she didn't. Her reply was that she was lacking in something and that if she had it, things would have turned out better. This is very interesting, because not only does she believe she has done something wrong, she also believes there is something wrong with her. I asked if it was really true that she could have done something other than the thing she did. I suggested that if she could have done something different she would have.

There is a strange misapprehension about time in all this. In effect, this woman is saying that if she could rewind time she would have done something different, but clearly neither she nor anyone else has this magical ability. What is done is done and is not reversible. This is not to say that in the future, in similar circumstances, she will necessarily do the same thing, but given the way she has dealt with and perceived this event, it becomes very likely that she will in fact do exactly the same thing. Embedded in all this is the idea that there is something wrong with her. This alone is the most likely reason that the past will be repeated.

If we drop a cup and it breaks, is this reversible? It appears ridiculous to even ask this question, but what is the difference between the example of a broken cup and something we believe we could have done differently? This may all sound obvious, but is it?

Ask yourself if you have done what this woman does. Do you believe that you are someone who makes mistakes that should not have happened? I believe most of us do this. What is really going on? The truth is that all of us are actually doing the most that it is possible in that moment.

How we react or respond to a situation is determined by the information we have accumulated about ourselves. Much of this information is flawed in that there may be a hidden belief that we are not good enough.

This is usually caused by the words or actions of others who, because they do not feel lovable, project this on to others. When we receive a projection like this, we usually accept it, because as children we have no defence against this false information and do not have the ability to discern what is true and what is false. The child trusts that the information he or she receives must be true. Once we have stored and believed a certain amount of this false information, something new begins to occur. When someone rejects us in any way, we are reminded of all the stored and believed information that we already hold. This stored information then erupts into the present, causing chaos.

Lets go on a journey, back to the beginning of the universe and the Big Bang. There is a huge explosion and, in time, matter is formed and flung out away from its point of origin. As time goes by, this matter undergoes many transformations, sometimes cooling and at other times sparking into life, such as when stars are born. At some point, the star that is our sun is born and around it there are clusters of matter that slowly forms into worlds. One of these worlds, the third nearest to the sun is totally inhospitable to life. Its atmosphere is toxic and the surface runs red with molten lava. After many millions of years, the Earth begins to cool down and conditions change. There is water and slowly the atmosphere becomes less poisonous. In time, somehow life begins to form. At first this life is very simple but it becomes ever more complex. This early simple life will ultimately reach a point in which it will be able to write about itself on a computer, as I am doing now. There is much that happens and needs to happen before this point is reached. This point is the moment we inhabit right now.

At certain points in history, it can be seen that all events are predetermined by all previous events. Nothing can happen in isolation. It would be ridiculous to look at early life on earth and wonder why there are no computers or aeroplanes or houses. The time has not yet occurred in which these things can exist. Likewise, to look at mankind and wonder why are we so aggressive to each other is ridiculous; we are not yet ready to be anything else.

What happens now is determined largely, if not solely, by what happened before. What happens now is the product of all previous events. Everything is as it should be and in fact could be no other way than it is. This may seem to be a nihilistic world in which anyone can do anything that they wish, but it is not that simple. It is not that we can do anything that we wish, but that we are largely programmed to behave in very particular and often predictable ways. Also, this process of all previous events determining the present event is still in operation. We are responsible in the sense that what we do, even though it may be determined by the past, still causes a result. This result may be experienced in the form of pain or pleasure. For instance, if I cause harm in any way to another, there will be a consequence that clearly will affect the other person but that will equally affect me, although this effect may be more subtle.

We are all of us immersed in this process in which what we do is largely determined by the past, but what we do has consequences that are then thrown into the mix. As a result of this we will slowly begin to adapt what we do. This process is a very slow laborious process, in which we tend to learn from our mistakes only after having experienced the negative result of our actions many times. The culmination of all Karma, in essence, is that whatever we do is determined by the past and we cannot be held responsible for the past. Even though we are not responsible for the past, we must still face the consequences of our actions. A major principle to come out of this is that all people at all times are always doing the best that they possibly could do in every moment. Others observing what people do may decide that people are bad, wrong or even evil. This cannot be so; we can only act according to the information that we have available. If our information is flawed or missing then we can only act according to the information we have. Again, just because the information we have is flawed or missing, does not mean that we are exempt from the consequences of our actions.

15. Will the Real God Please Stand up?

A client told me about his friend who had recently died. He felt guilty and said that he should have done more to help. He knew that in the past his friend had been addicted to drugs and, although he had been able to stop for a while, he suspected that his friend had returned to his habit. His friend had died of hepatitis through sharing a needle. I told him about a friend of mine who had committed suicide many years ago. Long before my friend committed suicide, I had felt that this would be his final solution. Over the years, I tried to help and warned him directly of where he was headed. He was unable to hear me. Could I have done more? I don't know, but I feel in some way there was a destiny being acted out.

I recently saw a film called *Bartleby*, scripted from a story by Herman Melville. In the film, Bartleby is a clerk who is generally good at his job, but on occasions when asked to do something, he would hesitate and then say 'I would prefer not to'. As the story unfolds, this behaviour increases. More and more often when he is requested to do something, he says 'I would prefer not to', and there seems no apparent reason why he chooses to do some things but not others. In time, he reaches the point where he prefers to do nothing at all. Finally he keels over and dies. This film is about a man whose life has no meaning. He chooses to do some things but not others, for no apparent reason. As time goes on, he does less and less – and then he dies. Does this story sound familiar to you? Are you choosing for no apparent reason some things over others? Are you living a life without meaning? Is the meaning of life to do with the work or career we choose? Is it to do with our family or friends? Is it about getting rich or famous, or is it perhaps striving towards some political or spiritual ideal? Maybe meaning is to do with power, to feel powerful or to hold power over others. Maybe it's in having as good a time as possible until we die. This last meaning is very popular. Most of what we find to make sense of our lives come from one or more of the above. Do animals have or need to do this? I doubt that they think too much about this question.

One day I noticed our family cat stretched out on my son's bed. I went over to look at her. She seemed completely relaxed and playful. Two hours later, she was dead for no apparent reason other than old age. As I watched her on my son's bed earlier, it would not have occurred to me that within two hours she would be dead. For me, the meaning here is not about the death of our cat – it is about how that death touches myself, my partner, and my children. The relaxed playful cat is no more, but we still exist and feel. The death touches me, but I know it will touch my children and my partner more.

Recently while running my psychotherapy group, something happened that I think took everyone by surprise. A group member David began talking about finishing his job. Some conflict had occurred between him and his boss. It seems that they had both decided that it was not working and that David should leave. David was talking very reasonably about this, saying things like 'it was for the best' and 'I was not really happy there'. I and others in the group commented that there was not much feeling in what he was saying. Suddenly, David began crying, but this was no ordinary crying. To my ears, it was the crying of a deeply hurt child. This was not crying from self-pity – rather it was more akin to a howling that was emerging from his body without any conscious volition.

At one point David stopped crying and asked 'what was that sound'? David later said he was not aware of what it was that was causing him to cry.

It is easy enough to give meaning to these events, but what comes before meaning is feeling. For me, the feeling is the meaning. I am not looking for anything else. When we add meaning to feeling, the feeling is diminished and repressed. If we hurt, it is natural to feel.

I was talking to someone about meditation and he said the difficulty for him was in doing something (meditation) without measurement. There are no apparent signposts or markers to say what we have achieved or not achieved. It is like being in a desert and not knowing which way to go, except that we need to go on or die. This is one of the reasons that meditation is so difficult for so many people; we are faced with a world of unknowing. In the beginning, we try to impose meaning on the world.

We want to know how we are doing, so we tell ourselves exactly how we think we are doing. We may tell ourselves that we are pretty close to being enlightened or perhaps we think we have finally cracked it and now we are enlightened. We may feel that we are failing dismally and surely that everyone else is doing better. In meditation, we are faced with a world without signposts and the same could be said for life. In the absence of meaning, we instinctively create it.

Our greatest fear is that our secret will be found out, the secret being the strange ideas we have conjured up in order to protect ourselves from an apparently uncaring world. Many people have a meaning that involves God. Often, this involves some concept of heaven and hell as well as punishment, sin, and enlightenment. Meanings regarding God tend to be very structured and there are hierarchies of attainment.

Meanings are stories we tell ourselves when we are afraid of the dark. Sometimes we tell ourselves stories about what we should fear that resides in the dark. With meaning we can forget for a while that we are afraid or in pain. We can also forget that we are responsible. We can look to some higher authority that will tell us what the meaning is and how we should behave. Isn't it strange that throughout history God has required a human messenger or interpreter? You would think that if there is something God requires of us, he would appear to us and say exactly what he wants. What we usually get is a human prophet, who in the secrecy of his or her own home communes with God and then tell us what it is that God wants.

Prophets throughout history have given their followers different rules and instructions, supposedly passed on directly from God. These followers then go on to form various religious organizations that can be very intolerant of other religions. How many gods are there and will the real God please stand up? I am not saying there is no God, but that there are too many versions of God. I do not trust someone who tells me what God is or what he wants. Why should I believe one god over another god, or one religion over another especially when the messenger is always human as I am? If I told you that I am a prophet and that God has spoken to me, would you believe me? If a child is always dependent on the 'father' to tell him or her how to behave and what to believe then that child is doomed to remain a child forever. I am not denigrating children, merely saying that being a child is not meant to go on forever.

16. Intolerance

As a psychotherapist, I have been talking to people for around 25 hours every week for the last 15 years. This is a lot of therapy, and as far as I am concerned, I am as much a recipient of this process as my clients. In the process of psychotherapy, I notice shifting patterns between my clients and me, and even between clients. What I mean by this last statement is that sometimes I notice groups of clients being concerned with the same issues at more or less the same time. I find that I have an opportunity to explore this issue in depth with each client. Each person has a slightly different viewpoint and this lends itself to this exploration.

Over the years, the word 'intolerance' seems to come up in many different ways. For instance, a client might tell me about their feelings about a partner who snores. Another may talk about their feelings of anger while driving, maybe because they perceive that someone is driving too slowly or that someone is tailgating them. Another example might be a partner who is not paying enough attention or maybe watches too much television. All of these are examples of intolerance and are very useful clues to the state of a person's consciousness and mental health. The degree of intolerance indicates the degree of that person's problems in the world. Intolerance is not a trait that we like to apply to ourselves and it is interesting how it is so often associated with religious beliefs. As individuals make up nations, nations also can be incredibly intolerant of other nations – or even of their own citizens.

Children in particular are subject to much intolerance. This is largely due to their inherent status, which is someone with little or no power; in this respect there would also be a difference between the perceived power of a boy or a girl. Here, then, is a fundamental rule which dictates intolerance. Intolerance is determined by the perceived power that one person holds over another. In every relationship, even between identical twins there is an inherent agreement as to who holds the power. We are always looking at the world from our own perspective of power. The minute we meet someone, we begin to scan them to determine if they are more or less powerful than ourselves.

Once this is established, we either behave towards this person in a slightly subservient manner or establish a dominance over them. It seems that in all relationships, one person will instinctively take the lead and the other will allow this – or even encourage the other person to do this by actively not making a choice. It is clear that we all experience someone taking the lead from the beginning, namely our parents. This is obviously necessary, yet at the same time it is here that the problems begin. If children are treated as though they are incapable of making choices or even of learning from their mistakes, they will begin to believe that they are indeed incapable of making choices or learning from their mistakes. Then, as the child becomes an adult, he or she will often seek out people or situations that reflect these early beliefs. Children themselves can be extremely intolerant, but again this is often because of the intolerance they have experienced.

I like to ask questions about things like this, such as, what could be the purpose of intolerance? As intolerance seems to be so universal, maybe there is a reason for this. Perhaps there is a biological purpose to it. The Romans, for instance, were so successful for so long because of their ability to work together towards a particular outcome. In battle, they fought with a degree of discipline that was unheard of at that time. Julius Caesar could lead and organise others to an extraordinary degree.

We could say that for these systems or organisations to work, there needs to be a certain degree of intolerance, which in essence means that some will lead and many will follow. The followers do not lead and the leaders will not tolerate the followers to lead, as this would result in chaos. Many of the tribes that the Romans fought failed for this very reason; there were too many leaders, all pulling in different directions. This was the same problem experienced by the American Indians. Throughout human history, this seems to have been the case; some are born to lead and many to follow.

Animals also appear to organise themselves into leaders and followers with the same intolerance required to achieve this. This all suggests that there is a biological principle at work here. If we look at a family, we see that there is a chain of command. It could be that the father or mother holds the most power. If the father holds the most power and makes bad choices, the family or those who follow will suffer.

Sometimes it may be that children hold the most power in the family, which does happen. Often this happens because the child perceives that the parents are ineffectual and that they are unable to lead with clarity or that they give in too easily to the child's demands. If some are born to lead and many to follow, and if this is based on a certain degree of intolerance, is it then acceptable to value intolerance as a useful human trait? There does seem to be an argument for this being the case. For instance, all countries in the world agree to drive their cars on one particular side of the road. Some countries prefer the left and others the right side. If there were no agreement on this, there would be chaos. But here again, a degree of intolerance is required; ultimately someone has to decide which side of the road to drive on. Anyone who disagrees may be punished. All laws could be thought of as laws of intolerance but it seems clearly to be of value in this instance.

Most countries and governments will not tolerate murder. However, there have always been those who will. Laws and any other kind of rule we may create need to be looked at on a regular basis to check that they are still there for the common good. On an individual level, intolerance involves everyone wishing to be a leader while more often than not pretending to be a follower. We work best when we work together in harmony for the common good. If someone has a better idea of how to do things, that person should be listened to.

In the world as it is, you are listened to if you have power and usually ignored if you do not. In the past, empires like Rome have fallen partly because power was not based on ability but on birth. If you were born into the right family, you were automatically given power and your ability was of very little importance. In recent centuries Great Britain has made this same mistake and even America, which claims the opposite, is still ruled by birth and money and not necessarily ability.

17. Madness?

I had been away on holiday and it was my first day back at work. I was working in a psychiatric unit for adolescents at the time and on entering the unit I found myself immediately in a world of chaos. I was not unfamiliar with chaos in this psychiatric unit, but this chaos seemed different somehow. Maybe it was just that I was in a different state after coming back from my holidays. As soon as I entered the unit, I was told by the nurse in charge to go upstairs and help out. I was not given a handover or any explanation of what was going on upstairs. The upper floor of this building was where the dormitories were located. I was told to go up to the girls' dorm. When I arrived upstairs, I was met by a number of nurses who looked like they had had a very rough day. All this chaos had been caused by the arrival on the unit of a fourteen-year-old girl. Since arriving, she had been completely out of control. Apparently she had been talking gibberish since her arrival and was running around, shouting and taking off her clothes and throwing them out of a window. No one seemed to know how to deal with this girl, apart from just watching her and making sure she did not harm herself. The more I heard this girl, the more convinced I became that there was an order or pattern to the words she was using.

Later in the shift, I spoke to the nurse in charge and told her I would like to try something. She was very happy to give my idea a try. We decided to take this girl into the gym with just me, the charge nurse and one other student nurse. In the gym, the girl continued talking gibberish. For a while we just listened then I began asking the girl some very simple questions. The questions were only to do with the language she was using. I found I was really interested in the language she was using as it sounded like a genuine language – but one that no one else knew. I believe my interest was transmitted to the girl with the result that she began to respond to my questions. Slowly, she became understandable, calmer and more rational. As I came to understand her language, it became possible to expand our dialogue to other areas. Within half an hour, this girl had moved from apparent 'madness' to being sensitive and intelligent.

For the rest of her time in the unit, she would use every opportunity to talk with me, always very intelligently and never again using her gibberish language. This girl had been brought up in a so-called spiritual commune where, from a young age, she had observed adults, including her parents, having sex in the name of free love. I have no doubt that this forced this young girl to escape into her own private world with her own private language. This incident forced me to question my perception of 'madness'. Very often when going through the case histories of young people admitted to the unit it was clear that they were in an intolerable situation in which they had no option but to find a suitably creative way to survive. Another example of this is a girl who said that her father was sexually abusing her and that her mother knew but did nothing to protect her. Here is a situation in which this girl has no one to turn to for help and to survive she feigns madness. Sometimes what we say is not believed and then actions speak louder than words. It is very easy for people to dismiss what this girl says, but not so easy to dismiss her crazy behaviour. The girl does not care how she gets help as long she gets it. In this instance, what she needs most is to be away from her father. This was something I saw time and time again: adolescents in intolerable situations being very creative and finding the help they needed – the most obvious being living part of their life in a psychiatric unit.

18. Only a Little Dust

The key to solving all human problems lies in how well we understand the nature of the ego. This is not that difficult to understand. Patanjali said that the mind itself could not be seen but that it is possible to see the qualities of the mind such as comprehension and incomprehension, sleep and memory. The same could be said about the ego; in itself it cannot be seen but in its actions it becomes crystal clear. The first action that reveals the existence of the ego is defence. When we experience any feeling that we would rather not experience, there is a strong possibility that a particular defence will be initiated. The ego does not wish us to feel anything that may remind us of something that we have buried in our past. This may be the belief that we are unlovable and, although we believe this with all of our being, we do not wish to be reminded of the fact. But why is the ego so afraid of experiencing the feeling that is connected to this fact? One reason is that if we were able to naturally experience feeling unlovable, there would be no reason to employ the ego to get rid of these feelings.

What happens when the ego becomes redundant? This can only happen when we are able to tolerate what we naturally feel. What we naturally feel can only be physical sensations. These only become a problem when we label them as anger, fear, anxiety, sadness, and happiness. All of these and more we believe we feel, but prior to using any of these labels is the actual physical sensation. Regardless of how well the ego defends us against these unwanted feelings and sensations, life will inevitably strip away all defences to reveal the underlying truth.

The mechanism involved in this stripping away is pain. Pain is not the problem we think it is; it is not pain that is the problem it is what we do to turn pain into suffering. What we do to turn pain into suffering is add meaning to physical sensation.

In the beginning, what we call anger is actually just physical sensation. Because we do not want these physical sensations, we try to control them and we do this by giving them meaning. Look at what happens when we turn physical sensation into anger. What started as an uncomfortable physical sensation now becomes a problem that can lead to violence, war and many other unpleasant situations. As long as we are defended against these unwanted feelings, this cycle will continue. You might think there are also positive feelings such as happiness. These are usually conditional and, because of this, not truly positive. Positive feelings are conditional in that they are dependent on satisfying our desires. If we don't get what we desire, we can become very unhappy and sometimes even depressed. We could even become suicidal.

We have the capacity to be very defended indeed and for it to appear that we have completely solved all of life's problems. Life is very patient, however, and is prepared to wait for the moment when we are least likely to expect it. Everything we hold dear can be taken away in a moment and there is nothing on earth we can do about it. Money, fame, power or God will not protect us. When that which we hold dear is taken away, there is the strong possibility of vulnerability. If we move towards being vulnerable, we can then begin to approach the truth. Another aspect of the ego is its inability to tell the truth, but what is the truth? When we approach this question using philosophy or religion we, are doomed to fail. Philosophy and religion are the products of the ego which is unable to perceive or tell the truth. When we try to answer this question using the ego, we will fail. It does not matter how the ego answers this question; it will always be wrong. It is only when the ego is suspended that the truth begins to emerge. What happens when someone whose ego is suspended speaks to someone whose ego has not been suspended?

This reminds me of something I heard Krishnamurti say during one of his talks at Brockwood Park. He said to his audience, 'if you understood what I was talking about, you would not be here'. He was telling us that we did not understand what he was talking about, not because of some inherent ignorance but because what he was saying could not be comprehended by the dominant part of our mind. If this was true, why was he talking at all to this audience and the people he had spoken to over many years? Why would you talk to someone if you knew beforehand that they would not understand what you were talking about?

Words similar to these were spoken more than 2,500 years ago. On being enlightened, Buddha said 'How can I tell anyone about what I have experienced, they would never understand'? At this point, an angel is said to have appeared and said to Buddha, 'there are some people with only a little dust in their eyes'. I realised that this also applied to what Krishnamurti said, he was not giving people information that he thought they would or would not understand; he was giving them information that was designed to disrupt the information they already had. Zen master Dogen did something similar about nine hundred years ago with his book *The Shobogenzo*. In this book, Dogen veers between passages of extreme lucidity to passages that seem to verge on nonsense. Reading this book, I feel that someone is drawing me in with the lucid passages. When I think I understand what is being said, he pulls the rug out from under me and I am left in a state of confusion. This I am sure is by design.

Many men and women, at different times in history, have attempted to disrupt the information that is taken to be true by others. Coming from a very different tradition and culture was Rumi, a Sufi poet and mystic who had a fairly similar style of writing, moving from great lucidity to the almost incomprehensible. Rumi used poetry to disrupt the information we take to be true. As with all these methods, they can only work when we are ready or in an open enough state, or when the mind has become less rigid in the way it views its own ideas.

19. Three Parables

More and more thinking becomes redundant. Why think when thinking serves no useful purpose? The problem here is that although thinking often does not serve any useful purpose, it does serve a non-useful purpose. That purpose is to do whatever it takes to ensure its own survival. To do this, it needs to convince you that without it (the ego) you will not survive. Preferably, it needs to convince you that you have a long-term problem, the longer the better – and preferably one that will take all of your life to solve. The ego convinces you that you have a problem, or problems, and convinces you that it is only the ego that could possibly solve these problems. Here is a short story I call 'The Parable of the Brick' that I use to illustrate how the ego plays this game.

The Parable of the Brick 1

Imagine a man walking along a road. Suddenly he trips over a brick lying in the road. He picks himself up and continues walking. A few hours later, this man comes back the same way and again trips over the brick. Again, he picks himself up and continues walking. This man continues tripping over the same brick every day and this continues for many years.

Here is another version.

The Parable of the Brick 2

Imagine a man walking along a road carrying a brick. Suddenly he puts the brick down, walks back a few steps, walks forward and trips over the brick. The man continues to do this wherever he goes.

If you were observing this, what would you think? Surely you would think this man is crazy. In the first version, the man seems to not notice the brick and so falls over it. In the second version, not only does he obviously see the brick, he puts it down and purposely trips over it. Continuing to trip over the same brick would be very strange, but carrying the brick with him placing it in his own path and then tripping over it is downright crazy.

These two parables are two ways of viewing what most people are doing for most of their lives. In the first, we are not paying attention and so continue to make the same mistake, potentially for many years. In the second, it is more than not paying attention it is more like self-sabotage. If this man were paying attention, he could never trip over the brick. This is an important clue showing how we can begin to solve this problem. We are not paying attention and the reason for this is that we are too busy thinking about ourselves. Being too busy thinking about ourselves is called 'neurosis', a very common western ailment. We are so busy thinking about ourselves that we literally can't see what is directly in front of us. This only partly explains the behaviour of the man in the second parable. Why would we sabotage ourselves, in this purposeful way? This kind of self-sabotage can only occur if there is an unconscious desire to punish ourselves, which could only happen if we feel unlovable.

I have seen many examples of both these behaviours over the years in my psychotherapy practice. I have also had to suffer the consequences of behaving this way myself. I use another story that I call 'The Parable of the World in Chaos', to illustrate more clearly what the problem is and where the solution lies.

The Parable of the World in Chaos

Imagine that you step outside of your front door and immediately you are in a world of danger. There are huge holes everywhere. If you were to fall down one of these holes. you would die. There are obstacles and sharp objects everywhere. There are wild animals roaming about, waiting to pounce on anyone not paying attention.

This is not so dissimilar to a world we once all lived in; a Darwinian world in which only the fittest survive. This world still exists in the Amazon rainforest for the tribe I mentioned earlier. At the age of about three, children are expected to begin fending for themselves and they begin helping the adults in hunting and gathering. They are still loved but no longer mollycoddled. This is very painful for them as the change is very abrupt. If they survive, these children grow up to be very sturdy and resourceful hunters and gatherers.

Death is quite commonplace in this environment and a woman having a breech birth is left to die with the tribe just watching; no one goes to her aid, no one even consoles her. This is indeed a world of chaos, but for these people it is the world they live in.

Here is another example. On my second trip to India, a friend and I had managed to find a lift with someone who was driving there. While driving through Iran, we picked up a man looking for a lift to Afghanistan. This man could speak many languages and seemed to live a very nomadic kind of existence; he appeared to me to be well educated, although I would guess this education did not occur in any school or university. While driving through a desert area of Iran, we decided to camp out in the desert overnight and continue on our journey the next morning. On waking up the next morning, we began to prepare breakfast. While doing this, I noticed a black dot out in the desert moving in our direction. As it got closer, the black dot turned into a young boy. I was mystified; why was a young boy walking out of the desert? As the boy got closer, I could see that he was not going to approach us; he appeared to be headed towards the city of Teheran. I decided to go and talk to the boy. The man we had picked up came with me. It turned out that the boy was from Afghanistan and was about twelve years old. He could not speak English but the man translated for me. I asked through my interpreter what the boy was doing in the desert and where he was from. The boy explained that he had walked from Afghanistan to Iran because his family was poor; he had walked to Iran in order to find work so that he could take money back home and help his family. He had found a job with a baker in Tehran but had nowhere to live, so each night he walked out into the desert and slept in a hole in the ground. The world we live in couldn't be more different; we live in a world of luxury and safety in comparison to the Amazonian world and this boy's Afghani world.

So what do we do in response to this luxury and safety? We attempt to create our own danger. We become neurotic, which is dangerous, because when we are neurotic we are no longer paying attention. We smoke and drink and take drugs, we overeat and undereat, drive too fast or drive too slow. Many will risk their lives climbing mountains, free-fall parachuting and driving racing cars; the list is endless.

We still wage war at every opportunity and allow millions to die of starvation. All of this can be seen as the ego's attempt to keep us in chaos and danger. I am not suggesting we all go and live in the Amazon rainforest or Afghanistan, but clearly this world of safety we have created in the west has many unforeseen problems. Living in a dangerous environment forces us to pay attention. Can we learn to pay attention without living in this way? Yes, but that brings us back to meditation which for the ego is a dangerous environment. Even though the ego is fearful of this environment, it is actually safe. Although the ego is afraid of losing its power, this isn't a problem as it doesn't really exist. Meditation in the beginning is difficult and requires some effort but eventually it can lead us to a state of constant awareness without difficulty or effort.

20. Sound

Here is a very useful and gentle form of meditation, given on a retreat.

From the moment you wake up until the moment you are asleep, focus your attention on all the various sounds that fill your world. Allow all your other senses to fade into the background. Just for today, hearing will be your dominant sense. As with sitting meditation, the moment you become aware that your mind has wandered, gently return your attention to hearing. Imagine you have been deaf since birth and all of a sudden you can hear. I remember seeing a news item on television where a woman who had been deaf since birth had an operation to allow her to hear for the first time. Every sound filled her with excitement and joy, and while listening to some music she cried. Imagine your world suddenly filled with sound for the first time. Even when it seems very quiet, there are sounds to be heard.

When someone is speaking, listen carefully to the tone and the speed of the speaker.

Try to do two things at the same time; listen with attention and understand the meaning of what is being said. At the same time, focus your attention on the actual sound itself. During the walking meditation round the lake, hear all the sounds around you; the birds singing, the sound of the wind and the two small waterfalls. See if it is possible to hold your attention on the sound of the water all the way around the lake.

Try to keep your focus on hearing all through the day while meditating, eating and during all other activities of the day. Finally, at the end of the day, keep your focus on hearing all the way, into sleep and even during sleep.

21. The Abyss

One of my psychotherapy clients told me that during his working week he feels tired but OK. When his working week ends on Friday evening, he suddenly finds that he is not OK. He told me he feels a sense of emptiness and that his life has no meaning. As he spoke, I recalled a film I had seen the previous weekend, *The Assassination of Richard Nixon*, a rather dark and depressing film. The film seemed to me to be about a man whose life is slowly drained of all meaning. As it progressed it became clear that this man was one of life's failures; he tries hard but somehow everything he does fails. His marriage had broken up and he felt despair in his work as a salesman. He feels this way because he is expected to lie to customers and because he feels unable to be true to himself. He planned to start his own business based on truthfulness, but this never got off the ground. He was out of sync with everyone around him and he slowly began to disintegrate. In one scene this man was speaking into a microphone connected to a tape recorder. He talked about being a grain of sand, and that he had no power or meaning. He also said that he is one of 200,000,000 other grains of sand – referring to most other Americans. He began to focus on Richard Nixon, whom he perceived as someone who has power and formulated a plan to assassinate him. He believed that assassinating someone who has power is the only way for him to get power.

Suddenly, I understood something I thought I already had understood. Understanding has many levels and, although I may think I understand something completely, there usually comes a time when I hit a new level and my understanding deepens. This was such a time; suddenly I understood something that applied not just to my client but also to myself and everyone else. What is it that happens to my client every Friday night? What happens is that his defence of distracting himself temporarily collapses, but not for long, he soon implements another defence, alcohol. What is he distracting himself from? What are the feelings he has when he is no longer able to use work as a distraction? We might call these feelings boredom, a feeling of emptiness; a sense that life has no meaning or that somehow we are worthless and unlovable. Let us call this state 'the abyss'.

This state is who we really are; something akin to annihilation. All our worst fears and a most profound sense of desolation reside here.

Imagine a room that is divided in the middle by an invisible wall. On one side of the room, the left hand side is where this state of desolation resides. On the right hand side of the room is the world of our distractions. This is where we conjure up all the different worlds we inhabit that keep us distracted from the abyss. The invisible wall and the right hand side of the room is the domain of the ego. The ego's purpose is to make sure that we never experience the abyss. In the right hand side of the room is the infinite potential for distraction. In this side of the room, we can devise new distractions. Here is a short list of some of these distractions.

- Power – most of the human race is very busy inventing new ways to attain this, consciously or unconsciously.
- Pleasure – all the various pleasures involved in satisfying the mind and the body.
- What we call mental illness – including neurosis and depression.

- Greed, anger and illusion – these last three are the distractions as seen by Buddhists.

All distractions ultimately arise from these Buddhist distractions; greed, anger and illusion. These three are actually one, as greed and anger arise out of illusion. A distraction is when the mind chooses to focus its attention on one thing, thereby removing its attention from something else. Faced with the sense of annihilation in the left hand side of the room, we begin to appreciate any distraction that can refocus the mind away from this perceived threat. As can be seen, this list covers most of human activity. This is not to say that all these things in themselves are distractions; only that all of them can be used as distractions. All of these distractions are usually seen as necessary and good, unless we take them too far. Clearly, no matter what we do within the confines of the right hand room has nothing whatsoever to do with what is real; it is an escape from what is real. What is real can only be found in the left hand side of the room.

What is real is not the abyss, although to get to what is real we must first pass through it. The abyss is still illusion; it is the ego saying here is something I don't like and so I will name it 'abyss' or any other variation of this, and in so doing feel that I have some control. Again, this is the ego telling us what is real and what is not. The ego is not able to tell us what is real – it can only tell us what is not. In the two-room analogy, there is not a third room; there is only one room in the first place and everything is contained and created in and from this one room. This room is consciousness itself and everything in the room, including, all the above, is also consciousness itself. As long as we think there are different sides of the room and different things contained in the room, we are trapped. We are trapped in a room of our own creation.

What sound does a tree make when it falls in the forest and there is no one there to hear it? Not only is there no sound; there is no falling, no tree and no forest. Without consciousness, none of these can exist. I am writing about a tree falling in a forest but these are just words – and without consciousness, who is reading or writing these words?

You could say that, just because there is no one around to see and hear the tree falling, does not mean that there is not a tree falling. But there is no tree falling, that is just a story and can only be conceived within consciousness.

22. Stories That Define Reality

Before we describe how and why stories define reality, let us first define what a story is. A story can be defined in a number of ways, but at the root it is a series of ideas based on language. Language is composed of words, and words contain sounds or signs that are used to represent or re-present some aspect of reality. The word 'apple' and all other words associated with that word such as 'green', 'round' or 'delicious' are essentially just a clever trick we have learned that allows us to agree with others as to the use and meaning of things. It may be this one trick that has more than any other enabled the human race to achieve the many wonders of modern technology, art, music and architecture. At the same time, it has backfired and also produced such things as war, crime, mental illness, addictions and greed.

How is it that something as simple as a word could be responsible for all the positive and negative attributes of the human race? The reason is based on a simple misunderstanding of language. Over many thousands of years, and within many cultures, the word has become godlike, in that the word and the reality have become confused one with the other. When these words occur in our mind, they are not just words that are used to represent reality they may become reality. Quite often, I come across people who appear angry. As I get to know them, I see that they are angry but that they believe that others cause their anger. Children often express their feelings in this way when they say that someone has made them angry. If one becomes angry it must be that something is being believed that is not true. The form this belief usually takes is 'it shouldn't be like this'. If it is a belief, then it must also be formed of ideas and language, either spoken or thought. If words were not taken to be real or true, they could have no effect.

I remember reading a book by J. Krishnamurti many years ago, in which he said 'It is not that we are angry but that we are anger itself". As usual with Krishnamurti, this statement forced me to use my mind in a way that I was not used to doing. On the surface, this statement sounds as though 'we are angry' and 'we are anger itself' are the same, but there is a subtle and crucial difference.

When someone talks about being angry, or just by observing someone who is angry, we can see that they believe that their anger is caused by something outside of themselves. If we see that we are anger itself then the world has done a complete about-turn. There is no cause outside of me, although there are certainly things outside of me that can trigger the reality that I am anger. What does 'I am anger' mean? It means that the anger I experience is not caused outside of me but has its origin inside. Furthermore, this reality inside of me is something that has probably been with me for a long time and something that I take with me wherever I go. We have all seen people who seem always to be angry; they tell themselves and they tell us that others cause this but it is not true. The anger has been there a long time and can only be re-awakened by others.

How does all of this connect to the way we use words and language? When we are anger itself we deny this by shifting the responsibility onto something or someone external to ourselves. In other words, we tell ourselves a story, a fiction about what is taking place in reality. As I said earlier this is a complete denial of reality. A story is a fiction and is never true. Therefore, the problem can never be solved as long as this way of looking at the world continues. This last statement applies to many other problems we are faced with; if something is not true then it cannot be made to be true just by saying it. Truth has nothing to do with language; we just use language to approximate some aspect of reality but invariably get this simple fact confused.

The fictions we can tell ourselves about reality are endless; there are many possible subjects. A story is a verbal or ideological way of describing something, or something that does not exist in any way other than the medium used to describe or tell it. For instance, these words I write at the moment are only pixels on a computer screen; they do not exist in any other way. They have no other relationship to reality and, unless you attach meaning to them, they have no possible purpose. In essence, a story is a fiction which may have a useful purpose or not.

Here are two simple examples to clarify what I mean by a useful or non-useful fiction.

I don't trust my girlfriend and I think that she may be having an affair with another man.

Someone approaches me and asks me the way to the nearest tube station.

In the first example, let us first establish that what is written or said is a fiction regardless of whether or not it is useful. A story is always a fiction because it is always a way of describing reality rather than reality itself. When I write the word 'apple' it may cause a response in you that evokes pictures, smells, or tastes that are associated with this word. But actually no apple is to be seen, smelled or tasted anywhere in reality – reality being the world as it is in this present moment.

If I ask you to imagine taking a bite of a lemon, this may produce quite a physical response in the sense that this particular use of language causes us to associate these words with a memory. This memory may be so vivid that even though there is no lemon to be seen or tasted, we may find that it stimulates our salivary glands. In the same way, when something is said or done that evokes a memory of anger, we physically feel a very subtle sensation in our body that causes us to believe in something that is not actually there. It is largely because of these physical sensations that the stories we tell ourselves can be so overwhelming and difficult to resolve.

Here is a story that was sent to me as an email. I do not know if this story is true or where it originally came from. True or not, there is no doubting the power of these words.

What would you do? You make the choice. Don't look for a punchline; there isn't one. Read it anyway. My question is: would you have made the same choice? At a fundraising dinner for a school that serves children with learning disabilities, the father of one of the students delivered a speech that would never be forgotten by all who attended. After extolling the school and its dedicated staff, he offered a question: 'when not interfered with by outside influences, everything nature does, is done with perfection. Yet my son, Shay, cannot learn things as other children do. He cannot understand things as other children do. Where is the natural order of things in my son? The audience was stilled by the query. The father continued, 'I believe that when a child like Shay, who was mentally and physically disabled comes into the world, an opportunity to realise true human nature presents itself, and it comes in the way other people treat that child.'
Then he told the following story:
Shay and I had walked past a park where some boys that Shay knew were playing baseball. Shay asked, 'do you think they'll let me play?'

I knew that most of the boys would not want someone like Shay on their team, but as a father I also understood that if my son were allowed to play, it would give him a much-needed sense of belonging and some confidence to be accepted by others in spite of his handicaps. I approached one of the boys on the field and asked (not expecting much) if Shay could play. The boy looked around for guidance and said, 'We're losing by six runs and the game is in the eighth inning. I guess he can be on our team and we'll try to put him in to bat in the ninth inning.' Shay struggled over to the team's bench and, with a broad smile, put on a team shirt. I watched with a small tear in my eye and warmth in my heart. The boys saw my joy at my son being accepted. In the bottom of the eighth inning, Shay's team scored a few runs but was still behind by three. In the top of the ninth inning, Shay put on a glove and played in the right field. Even though no hits came his way, he was obviously ecstatic just to be in the game and on the field, grinning from ear to ear as I waved to him from the stands. In the bottom of the ninth inning, Shay's team scored again. Now, with two outs and the bases loaded, the potential winning run was on base and Shay was scheduled to be next at bat. At this juncture, would they let Shay bat and give away their chance to win the game? Surprisingly, Shay was given the bat. Everyone knew that a hit was all but impossible because Shay didn't even know how to hold the bat properly, much less connect with the ball. However, as Shay stepped up to the plate, the pitcher, recognising that the other team was putting winning aside for this moment in Shay's life, moved in a few steps to lob the ball in softly so Shay could at least make contact, The first pitch came and Shay swung clumsily and missed. The pitcher again took a few steps forward to toss the ball softly towards Shay. As the pitch came in, Shay swung at the ball and hit a slow ground ball right back to the pitcher. The game would now be over. The pitcher picked up the soft grounder and could have easily thrown the ball to the first baseman. Shay would have been out and that would have been the end of the game. Instead, the pitcher threw the ball right over the first baseman's head, out of reach of all team mates. Everyone from the stands and both teams started yelling, 'Shay, run to first! Run to first!' Never in his life had Shay ever run that far, but he made it to first base. He scampered down the baseline, wide-eyed and startled. Everyone yelled, 'Run to second, run to second!' Catching his breath, Shay awkwardly ran towards second, struggling to make it to the base. By the time Shay rounded towards second base, the right fielder had the ball. The smallest guy on their team who now had his first chance to be the hero for his team. He could have thrown the ball to the second-baseman for the tag, but he understood the pitcher's intentions so he, too, intentionally threw the ball high and far over the third-baseman's head. Shay ran toward third base deliriously as the runners ahead of him circled the bases toward home. All were screaming, 'Shay, Shay, Shay, all the way Shay'. Shay reached third base because the opposing shortstop ran to help him by turning him in the direction of third base and shouted, 'Run to third! Shay, run to third!' As Shay rounded third, the boys from both teams and the spectators, were on their feet screaming, 'Shay, run home! Run home!' Shay ran to home, stepped on the plate, and was cheered as the hero who hit the grand slam and won the game for his team. 'That day', said the father softly with tears now rolling down his face, 'the boys from both teams helped bring a piece of true love and humanity into this world'.

Shay didn't make it to another summer. He died that winter, having never forgotten being the hero and making me so happy, and coming home and seeing his Mother tearfully embrace her little hero of the day.

AND NOW A LITTLE FOOT NOTE TO THIS STORY:

We all send thousands of jokes through the e-mail without a second thought, but when it comes to sending messages about life choices, people hesitate. The crude, vulgar and often obscene pass freely through cyberspace, but public discussion about decency is too often suppressed in our schools and workplaces. If you're thinking about forwarding this message, chances are that you're probably sorting out the people in your address book who aren't the 'appropriate' ones to receive this type of message Well, the person who sent you this believes that we all can make a difference. We all have thousands of opportunities every single day to help realize the 'natural order of things. So many seemingly trivial interactions between two people present us with a choice: do we pass along a little spark of love and humanity or do we pass up those opportunities and leave the world a little bit colder in the process? A wise man once said every society is judged by how it treats it's least fortunate amongst them. You now have two choices: 1. delete 2. Forward. May your day be a Shay Day.

Cinema, theatre, and literature do not have any impact on us without the physical sensations that are induced in us by sounds, images, or words. In the cinema, all that is really happening is that we experience patterns of light or sound in a darkened theatre, or equally on our television set in our living room. Clearly, certain patterns of light and sound in this sense can cause us to cry, laugh or feel afraid – when in actual reality nothing is happening to cause it other than a very clever deception. We are told a story using visual images and words designed to evoke a particular mental and physical response. In film making, if these elements are skilfully assembled then we may cry, laugh or feel afraid. If they are not skilfully assembled then we may just feel bored, which is still a response to something that is not there.

My first example of a useful or non-useful fiction was. I don't trust my girlfriend and I think that she may be having an affair with another man. Is the first statement useful fiction or not? The reason this fiction is not useful is that the statement made is not based on fact but on assumptions. This is not to say that the girlfriend is not having an affair; it is just to say that right now I do not know. If I do not know, what is the purpose of speculation? In this case, the only purpose I can see is that the person making the statement for some reason desires to experience pain. This may seem like an extraordinary statement but let us look at it more closely.

When I hear someone use the word 'trust' I realise there is already a story here or a series of assumptions that may be totally incorrect. When someone says they don't trust someone, they usually mean that they do not trust themselves. What is it we don't trust about ourselves? In the statement 'I don't trust my girlfriend', what is really being said is, if it is true that she is having an affair, I will not be able to deal with the feelings or sensations that may arise in me, or I am unable to trust my response to reality. My girlfriend may or may not be trustworthy but what I don't trust is my ability to respond correctly if she is not trustworthy.

What is reality? Reality is what occurs in any given moment and only in that moment.

If what occurs is spoken about, then the words that are spoken are occurring in the moment they are spoken – but they do not in any way mean anything. They are just sounds that are heard or not heard. Any meaning that may be attached to the words must come after the moment and therefore have little to do with reality. These words and their meaning are either useful or they are not, but they are always stories and therefore fiction.

My second example of a useful or non-useful story was, someone approaches me and asks me the way to the nearest tube station. Being asked directions to a tube station or anywhere else falls into the useful fiction type of story. The question and the answer are not guaranteed to be useful but in general, this type of story has some useful and practical purpose.

Other examples would involve any two people conversing with the purpose of useful co-operation. Few of us could survive without this form of useful fiction. Most human interactions involve this form of fiction.

If all stories are fiction, it becomes imperative that we discern the useful from the non- useful stories we use. My work involves untangling the infinite variety of non-useful stories we tell ourselves. Before I could even hope to begin this work, it became necessary to untangle my own stories that were not useful. The best means I know of to do this involves what is usually called meditation. I say 'usually' because, in the light of what I have been saying, meditation becomes yet another story, and this particular story has more meanings than most. The words 'spiritual' and 'religious' are also story words and it is not difficult to see the endless parade of meanings we can attach to these. I will continue to use the word 'meditation' but will emphasise what I consider now to be a useful meaning. Meditation is just sitting and ultimately becomes anything we are doing in the moment; standing, walking, eating, working or any other form of activity that occurs in life.

To begin, it is best to start with just sitting. The reason for this is based on a simple formula – which is that when we are still, the mind tends to also move towards stillness. On the other hand, when there is any physical movement, the mind is stimulated into movement as well. In stillness, it is easier to see the many distractions conjured up by the mind. Just sitting means that we are not trying to do anything else. This may be the hardest activity, but in time it may become the easiest. Why it is so difficult is because even though this particular activity requires no thought or story, it is almost certain that thoughts and stories will occur. So why is this if we are only being asked to sit?

Thinking is not required in the act of sitting, yet we are certain to think. I am not suggesting that we try to stop ourselves from thinking; only that we observe this discrepancy between the instruction to just sit and the fact that in the beginning this seems to be impossible to do without thinking.

It is important to observe this and begin to notice what happens when we just sit. When we are faced with the simple act of sitting, we find the origin of the story. We find that the story arises without any apparent cause. If we are just sitting, what is the purpose of any story? If the story begins in such a simple act of just sitting, what happens when we are moving around in the world and having to deal with all the challenges that the world throws at us?

Everywhere I look, I see that almost everyone in the world is busy telling themselves stories of complete fiction about who they are, what they like and dislike, what they hate and love, what they find pleasurable and painful, what they think God is and what it is they think God expects of them. There are many stories of violence, sexuality, addictions and various states that are called mental illness (more stories). There are stories within stories within stories. It is true that in the beginning was the word. All stories must begin with a word and all stories must end with the ending of words – or the ending in the belief in stories.

23. Full Attention in the Living Moment

At any moment in time, we are experiencing the world and ourselves through a particular state of attention or awareness. This state is usually not constant; it fluctuates across a broad spectrum of possibilities. How we experience the world is based largely on this aspect of consciousness. What is this attention? Where does it come from and why does it fluctuate? There are some basic questions that arise when looking at this issue; do external factors, internal factors, or both, determine attention?

When I look back at my life, I see that I have inhabited many varied states of consciousness. For a long time, it seemed that this was in the lap of the gods and that there was nothing I could do about it. I had a certain state of consciousness and that determined the choices I made and the life I therefore lived. This was not pleasant; in fact, it was often extremely painful. I feel very fortunate that this state of affairs was brought to an abrupt end by my sudden close proximity to death. In the brief span of time that I spent fighting for my life in the ocean, I experienced a number of different states of consciousness all compressed into a very short duration of time. These states ranged from bewilderment through increasing states of confusion to enormous fear and panic, until finally these states could go no further.

There is only so much fear and pain that can be experienced and although these states can be prolonged, in the particular situation in which I found myself they were not. There was a limit to the amount of fear and pain I experienced. The limit involved the abrupt understanding that nothing that I or anyone else could do could affect the outcome of what was happening to me. This understanding did not involve thought; it occurred spontaneously as a result of seeing the simple fact that I was powerless and that there was no one around close enough to affect the outcome. What happened next has intrigued and mystified me for many years. Time suddenly appeared to stop and, because there was no time, there was no meaning.

This was very strange. I was experiencing the world as it is, without any particular meaning. It is not that I was unconscious or in some euphoric state due to reduced oxygen intake; what distinguished this state was the absolute clarity in which I was experiencing the world, even as I was drowning. It felt as though my mind was divested of everything pertaining to time. At this point, I was not aware of any fear or pain; there was absolutely no resistance in me to what was happening, just a crystal clear observation of being in the world at that particular time. Being in that state, there was no way to tell how much time had elapsed, but at some point I became aware of something right before my eyes that suddenly held out the possibility of survival. I do not recall thinking about the possibility of survival or even of wanting to survive. It seemed very natural to me to accept that possibility and to act upon it.

What I had seen, which I could not have seen while experiencing fear and panic, was that in the distance – maybe twenty feet away – was a coral reef. If I could reach it, I would probably be able to stand on it. Standing on the coral with my head barely out of the water, I waited till I got my breath back, then put the snorkel in my mouth (in my panic the snorkel had come out of my mouth and I had been unable to put it back) I then proceeded calmly and easily to swim back to the beach, stopping along the way and just floating, then proceeding again. The state of clarity did not leave me – at least not for another two weeks or so, and even then not completely. In those two weeks, my world was turned upside down and inside out. I was seeing the world from a completely new perspective; I felt I was seeing the world as it is rather than in the confused way I had previously seen it. Now there was stillness and attention. 'I' was no longer the focus of my attention. My perspective had changed in a simple but profound way; now I no longer saw myself at the centre of everything. I had been so concerned with my experiences in the world that I had completely lost track of how others might be experiencing their world. What had I been so upset about, anyway? What I had been so upset about was usually that others were not behaving in a way that corresponded to my ideas of how they should behave. Of course, everybody else also has these strange rules about how the world 'should' be. Why are these rules or ideas strange? They are strange because the world is as it is regardless of how I think it should be.

The world really does not pay too much attention to my ideas of how it should be. It is also the case that people do not pay too much attention to how I *think* they should be. 'All problems in this world relate to this simple misunderstanding.' I wrote this a few days after the massacre in Blacksville in the USA. As I watched the news, I saw a video recording of the killer and heard him talk about why he was doing what he was doing and who was to blame. It was clear to me that this man was enraged that other people were not behaving as expected. We can see an approximation of this in a two-year-old child; the child shows absolute fury and incomprehension that mother is not behaving in a way the child expects. The child usually grows out of this extreme state, but never completely. When the child grows up, he or she still looks at the world through this childish lens. As an adult, this way of looking at the world causes us to feel that somehow the world is not quite the way it should be. It seems to become our holy quest to correct this – through the use of self-deception or stories that better suit what we want.

In this present moment, what do you see? If you say or think anything at all about this then you quickly find that you are not in the present moment at all. Strangely, all that is continues to exist whether or not you think about it. When I think about what I am seeing then I am overlaying a kind of personal commentary over the truth. The truth is there, prior to thinking about something; it is there when I think about something and it is there after I have thought about something. This is a long-winded way of saying the truth and what I think are two different things. This is absolute; what I think can never be the truth.

Thinking and language have always had a very simple purpose; they enable us to communicate with each other and therefore greatly increase our ability to survive. When you focus your attention on an object, a duality is created. There is you, and there is the object on which your attention is focused. This movement and distance between you and the object is interesting. It seems we can focus on any number of objects, but somehow we never look at the source of that attention. It just seems to be taken as a matter of fact. But what is the source of this attention? Is the source of your attention different from the source of *my* attention? Is the source of attention subject to change? Is there ever a time when your attention does not exist?

While sleeping, we are not dead, but this duality between the object and me does not exist. Just because we are not aware of an object does not mean that we do not exist. Without an object, what is left is the source of our attention; it does not need an object in order to exist, because it exists prior to the object. What can be said about the source of attention? Nothing can be said, because if it is, a duality is created and we have moved away from the source. Is sleep the only time that the source of attention can exist free of the object? Normally when we focus our attention on an object, the source of our attention seems to be discarded while the object of our attention can become so absolute that we become totally dominated by the object. What this means is that when you think about something, the thing that you are thinking about can become so real that you are forced to act in accord with the thought. This is because the source of our attention is lost; we seem to be unaware that it is there in the first place.

What happens when the source of attention is separated from the object? Abiding in the source of attention allows one the possibility of finally being free from the domination of our thoughts. There is suddenly the possibility of being free of any object we can conceive of. What does this mean? First of all, let us consider the power of conceiving of objects. When I refer to 'objects' I am referring to the way that we name and give meaning to what we experience. Pain, for instance, is an object in this sense. How do we perceive pain? For most people, pain is something to be avoided and therefore something we do not like. Once we arrive at this conclusion regarding pain, what follows becomes quite predictable; we begin the many strategies designed to avoid or eliminate pain. These strategies may then take on a life of their own.

There seems to be no limit to the strategies we can use in order to avoid pain. Apart from the obvious ones such as alcohol and drugs, there are the more subtle such as denial and selective amnesia. No matter how crazy our ideas are, we seem to have an inexhaustible capacity to believe that we are right. We can tell ourselves we drink alcohol because we like it, and that seems to be enough to convince ourselves that we do not have a problem.

We could also tell ourselves that we are killing, raping or stealing from others because they deserve it; somehow, we come to the conclusion that others are less than we are. Other conceptions we may have can also have far reaching-consequences. We can conceive of birth and death, right and wrong and good and bad. We can conceive of religion, and once we conceive of anything to do with God (also a conception) we have attached our beliefs to the highest authority possible and anything we may do in the name of God cannot be disputed. It is always humans who say what God does or does not want. If we argue with this then we might be killed, imprisoned, or excommunicated. God in the hands of humans can be extremely dangerous. All wars, violence and crime of any kind, all religions and beliefs and many so-called forms of mental illness are just some of the possibilities that can arise in the act of conception.

If you have an idea that you believe to be true, how would you know if it is actually true or not? All it takes is that you believe it. It really doesn't matter if the idea is sane or not. As long as we are identified with our own thoughts, we have the capacity to commit any horror and believe that we are justified in our actions. Thought is important, but not when it is used in these ways. Thought is a tool that we may use when the need arises, although sometimes it would be truer to say that thought uses us. Thought can decide that life is too painful and that we should take drugs or alcohol to alleviate the pain. If all else fails, thought can decide that it would be better to kill oneself. It is necessary to find our way back to who we truly are, for if we do not this situation must continue – with inevitably disastrous results.

24. The Law of Absolute Right

'The law of absolute right' is a term coined by Richard Wetherill (1906 – 1989). The law of absolute right is similar to the law of gravity. Even if you have no understanding of the word 'gravity', there is never a time when you are not affected by it. If we disregard the law of gravity, we could be seriously hurt. This law seems to be inherent throughout the universe, even though its effects may be different in other parts of the universe. The law of absolute right says that if you disobey this law then you will be hurt. The hurt could be immediate or it could take many years to manifest.

So what is this law of absolute right? Who is it that determines that something is right and something is wrong? Answering the second question will help in answering the first question. The answer to the second question is nobody; in fact, this is one reason why we have been unable to understand or answer this question. The answer is not determined by anyone because it is a natural law.

We may refer to Newton's law of gravity, for instance, but we cannot say that gravity did not exist until Newton came along and observed and named it. Gravity existed long before Newton and continues to exist long after. We may come up with all sorts of theories to explain what it is and what it does, but none of these explanations changes the fact of gravity in any way. Similarly, the law of absolute right is not dependent on any person's particular view because it exists as a reality the same way that gravity does. How can we tell what is right and what is wrong? Actually, we already have this knowledge of what is right and what is wrong, but we often fail to act on it. If you stand facing the sun but find that you cannot see the sun because something is in the way, it does not mean that the sun is not there. Maybe a building is in the way of the sun and it might in time appear that there is no such thing as the sun. So what is it that gets in the way of our seeing 'the law of absolute right'?

Wetherill says that if what we say or do is 'right' we become 'rational, moral and peaceful'.

Here, Wetherill is in no way saying what the law of right action is, but he is saying something about the result of what happens when we align ourselves with right action. He is saying that when people live in accord with right action, they do not give, invite or take offence, and they are rational, moral and peaceful. We already know exactly what the law of absolute right is; it is just that we choose to override it.

If we are driving at 80mph on the motorway when the speed limit is 70mph, it is virtually impossible not to know this. Apart from the signs that tell us the speed limit, it was a part of the test we took that allowed us to drive in the first place. Clearly we do know what is right in this example, but we choose to override that knowledge. We can find all kinds of justifications but at no time do we not know that it is not right. You might ask if it matters that we are driving 10mph faster than the speed limit. In this example, it might not matter at all – or it might be the difference between life and death. There are, however, many other examples where the decision to ignore what we know of what is right and what is wrong has very serious consequences. We might also ignore the knowledge of what is right by taking drugs and alcohol or by stealing, raping, and killing.

When we steal, are we really unaware that what we are doing is wrong? No; we just hope that we will get away with it. There is the knowledge that it is wrong and underlying this is the knowledge of what is right. What is right is simply the absence of what is wrong. As we always know exactly what is wrong, all we need do is refrain from doing it and we are automatically immersed in absolute right.

All our actions have absolute consequences. These can be delayed in appearing or they may occur instantaneously. Regardless of when the consequence appears, we already know we have done something wrong, and if we did not ignore this information we would have some awareness of the ultimate consequence of our actions. Another question we may ask about absolute right is, 'what the conditions are in which absolute right is most likely to occur and the conditions in which it is least likely to occur?' The one condition that is most likely to result in absolute right is truth. Not some abstract idea about truth, but the truth of what is arising before our eyes right now.

What is occurring before my eyes right now is absolute truth. The moment I try to describe or explain what that is, it disappears. In the moment there is that which is.

If I say that it is raining, that is a reasonably accurate statement relating to what I perceive to be true. If I say that it is raining and that I do not like it, something very interesting has occurred. The first part of the statement remains reasonably true but now I have added on a subjective view. What is wrong with that, you may think? What is wrong is that now I perceive it is raining, and for some reason I am not able to accept the simple fact of this.

I decide that it is raining but that it should not be. What is it we feel when we don't like something? In the case of not liking that it is raining, the feeling is quite subtle – but even so it is not a comfortable feeling. If we decide there are many things we don't like, discomfort begins to grow. When I have the thought 'I do not like this', and if I have that thought often enough, a correlation occurs in the body that confirms the thought. The correlation is of course that the body actually does feel the physical approximation of the idea. This physical approximation of the idea is very real; it is not an idea any more, although its origin is in the idea.

We go through life accumulating more and more ideas of what we like and what we do not like, at the same time creating a physical correlation to all of these ideas.

Somewhere in this process, we begin to experience something that is more than the sum of its parts. For instance, if we tell ourselves often enough that we do not like certain things about the world or about oneself, we might begin to experience and be diagnosed with depression. If creating mental ideas about myself also happens to create a physical correlation that is connected to the mental idea, what might the consequences ultimately be? In a word, the consequence would be suffering in one or more of the many ways that humans suffer. The simple act of thinking 'I don't like this' could ultimately lead one to drink, smoke, take drugs, over-eat, under-eat and all manner of addictions. All of these could ultimately lead to illness, both mental and physical, and these in turn could lead to death.

Pain is a part of the law of absolute right. Sooner or later, any deviation away from absolute right moves inexorably towards absolute wrong and therefore towards pain. There is no escaping these laws. You can delay the results of them and you can pretend for a long time that they do not apply to you, but these laws, more than human laws, do not go away. You have always been subject to these laws and if you look carefully you will see that they are already working. Pain always teaches us that something about what we are doing or thinking is not quite right. From the beginning, pain teaches us to adjust. With physical pain, we usually learn and adjust fairly quickly. This is not usually the case with mental forms of pain, which are caused by wrong thinking. When we attempt to solve this form of pain, we resort to the ego. The ego is the originator of wrong thinking and that which is the cause of the problem cannot be used to solve the problem.

In history, we can see many examples of men or women who have denied these laws of absolute right. Dictators, for instance, do not tend to live to enjoy a comfortable retirement. Given enough time, all of them are seen for what they are. Future generations will see very clearly what we are and what we have done. This is not about blame because, strange as it may seem, no one is to blame. However, everyone is responsible, which simply means we have to live with the results of what we do and what we have done.

25. The Magic Formula

When experiencing extreme states of fear or anxiety, focus your attention on sound. Exclude all other senses from your mind and fix your attention on any sound occurring around you. Do not think about what you are hearing, just allow the sound to be received by the ears. Do this with your complete attention. Do this for just three minutes – longer if you wish, but three minutes is usually sufficient. If fear or anxiety recurs, continue with the above formula. If you find this difficult, persevere. With practice, it becomes an easy and a relaxing thing to do.

The basic principle behind this is that fear and anxiety require the duration of time to exist. If you are hearing any sound with complete attention in the present moment for that moment time does not exist – and neither do fear or anxiety. I find the sense of sound tends to work best for this practice but you may find working with one of the other senses works better for you. The principle is the same: your complete attention in the present moment on whichever sense you choose.

26. The Spiral of Stillness and Attention

On my meditation retreats, I usually suggest that on meditation walks people focus their attention on one particular sense. I might suggest that people focus all their attention on their sense of vision and for the period of the meditation walk, allow all the other senses to fade into the background. During a meditation retreat, we begin to learn how to still the mind and to focus the attention more deeply. When stillness and attention are applied to focusing the mind on one particular sense, such as sight, we begin to increase our intake of information. This increase is experienced as a greater awareness of what our eyes are actually seeing. We begin to see much greater detail and to notice things that we previously would have not.

On a week retreat, I would suggest that people focus on one sense throughout the day. The next day, I would suggest another sense to focus on such as hearing or touch. Each day, there is an increasing spiral of stillness and attention being applied to each of the senses. Towards the end of the retreat, we begin to experience this spiral of stillness and attention, almost as though we are experiencing the world for the first time – much as a child might experience it. The world of the senses is truly vast, and this vast information is something that we are always receiving – regardless of whether or not we meditate. The reason for meditation is partly to enable us to access the information we are already receiving and partly to end the constant daydreaming that we call 'thinking'. In this context, thinking can be seen to be a state in which our awareness is reduced.

Zen master Bankei referred to this often, reminding people of the vast amount of information they were receiving that they were usually unaware of. This information that he referred to is what arises and passes in every instant. In each moment, we experience the world as it is through our senses. Our senses do not require thought, although this is an option. We seem to believe that what we experience can only be experienced when we think about or deliberate on what we are experiencing. Bankei referred to that which receives and processes this information as the 'unborn Buddha mind'.

Another example of the information we are receiving but unaware of is within the body itself. If we look at any simple action of the body such as walking, and look deeply at what is going on, we see a seemingly infinite number of actions and responses that are happening all beyond our conscious awareness. If we were to look deeper still to the molecular level of interactions within the cells of the body, this simple act of walking begins to appear truly miraculous. Obviously, it is unnecessary for us to be consciously aware of most of this information. In fact, it is essential that we filter out all the information that is not absolutely necessary.

This is where the conscious mind comes in. The unconscious can be seen as an almost superhuman – like level of information. This is the level of information that a very young child is receiving, but clearly this has to change. If this did not change, the child would remain a child and ultimately could not survive without help from others. It is necessary for the child to diminish the amount of information it is receiving. Parents and society ensure that this takes place by helping the child to filter out information from the unconscious field. The child learns that things have names and that the child itself is a thing and has a name. All of this is a diminishment of consciousness, but it is often seen as an expansion of consciousness.

This process of diminishing consciousness starts from the moment we are born and continues until we die. We start off with this superhuman amount of information that as the years go by steadily decreases until we develop more and more rigid ways of thinking which could ultimately result in senility. Long before senility, our minds can start to become narrow and rigid. Examples of diminishment of consciousness are racism, sexism and religious intolerance.

Obviously, there is a need for us to diminish our consciousness and wonderful things can be achieved from this and from an ability to focus. There is a fine balance required so that we have the ability to diminish consciousness and focus on fine details, while also having the ability to allow all the information in and therefore be able to see the bigger picture. This is very similar to the idea of process and content.
In psychotherapy, I see that most people have problems because they focus on content or details and seem unable to see the bigger picture or process. Content tends to be circular, as when a married couple blame each other for the problems they are having. The bigger picture or process usually clarifies what the real problem is. This is never one of the details. It may be that the bigger picture reveals that the reasons for the marriage are based on something that is not true, such as:

- This person is the man or woman of my dreams and everything will be wonderful from now on
- This person is rich so now I can live happily ever after
- This person is beautiful and sexy and now I can end my days in bliss
- This person is gifted and talented and maybe some of that will rub off on me

Marrying someone for any of these reasons could result in eventual disappointment. It is not that any of these details are wrong; it is just that a person is so much more than the details.

What you choose is what you get, so be very careful what you choose. The fact that what you are choosing may be unconscious to you makes no difference, because you will still get what you choose. You might want to consider these questions:

- Do I like this person?
- Is this person kind?
- Does this person love me as I am, without wanting to change me?
- Do I love this person without wanting to change him or her?

27. The Ultimate Fear

Someone in my psychotherapy group recently said that he thought his greatest fear was the fear of death. I responded by asking the group to brainstorm what they thought the ultimate fear might be. The group came up with a long list including the fear of loss of identity, life, pain, relationship, not existing, madness and many others. I said that I thought that our ultimate fear was none of these and that the fear is universal, because all human beings have the same ultimate fear. All other fears can be reduced down to this one root. The root fear is of the story that your mind tells you about everything. Reality is not about what happens outside; it is about what is created inside. What is created inside has little to do with what is happening outside. To concern ourselves with what is happening outside is a big mistake.

How is it that different people have such a varied perception of how they view the world? Living in the world and even living with the same general circumstances, we can have very different experiences, ranging from depression, fear and anxiety to joy, wonder and harmony. It is not the world that determines this, but what takes place within our own mind. This is where heaven and hell exist. In the world, heaven is considered to be the satisfaction of your desires and hell is not attaining these desires. Within the mind, the universe is created. What we see and experience is only what has been created in the mind. To not understand this must result sooner or later in suffering. This suffering is self-created and has no true reason to exist. To solve the problem of suffering, we must turn our attention inward rather than outward. We do not need to change our point of view from pessimistic to optimistic. Pessimism and optimism are yet more stories invented by the mind.

Certain physical sensations in the body are turned into stories by the mind. There is no limit to what these stories can be and whatever story we invent, we then have to live.

Stories also have the effect of further amplifying the physical sensations that started this process. A panic attack is a good example of this process. We look at the world and something in what we see causes us to feel uncomfortable. This uncomfortable feeling or physical sensation is then seized upon by the mind and turned into a story that suggests that what is seen that makes us feel uncomfortable will become more uncomfortable. As a result, the physical sensations become more intense, causing the story to become more fearful and this can continue until we are paralysed with fear.

Our greatest fear is our own ability to create all possible fears and the physical sensations that go with them. It could truthfully be said that these stories arise from nothing. There are no adequate words to describe this nothing. When we look for something, it helps if we know what we are looking for but not in this case. To have any idea of what we are looking for means that this 'nothing' has become something. For this reason, it is better to ask not what it is we are looking for, but what it is not. In Indian philosophy, this is referred to as 'neti neti' or ' not this, not this'. Can all fears reduce down to this one fear – the fear of our own imagination?

Here is a list of some of the possible stories we tell ourselves:

- I am depressed
- I am afraid
- I am anxious
- I am unlovable
- I am too old
- I am too young
- I am good
- I am bad
- I am ill
- I am mentally ill
- I am dying
- I am angry
- I am in complete harmony with all that is
- I am better than anyone else
- I am not good enough
- I am beautiful
- I am ugly
- I am enlightened
- I am clever
- I am stupid
- I am black
- I am white
- I am any other colour
- I am rich
- I am poor
- I am male
- I am female
- I am human
- I like...
- I don't like...
- I am an artist
- I am a Christian

- I am a Buddhist
- I am a Moslem
- I am a Quaker
- I am heterosexual
- I am homosexual
- I am a transvestite
- I am a sadist
- I am a masochist
- I believe in…
- I don't believe in…
- I am a saint
- I am a sinner
- I am English
- I am Indian
- I am Irish…

This list is endless.

For the story to be believable, it is necessary to establish proof to back up the story. This proof is usually in the form of another story. Let us look at one of these stories in detail to see how the story is constructed and reinforced. If I am a Christian, why am I a Christian? What if I had been born into a Moslem family? It is very likely that I am a Christian because the family I was born into were Christian with all the beliefs and rituals that go with that. I am not asked if I want this set of beliefs; they are imposed on me. My family and priest convince me that if I make a mistake, I am a sinner, but then of course in this system of belief I start off being a sinner. If I am told I am a sinner, I begin to feel guilt. Guilt is not just an abstract idea; it is made to feel real in the body with physical sensations. I do not need anyone else to convince me that I am a sinner because my own mind and body can do this quite adequately. Once I am convinced I am a sinner, I begin to see everyone else in the same light. Once I have the eyes of a sinner, all I see is sin. I begin to see other systems of belief as wrong because they are different to the ones I hold.

Of course, all of this applies equally to all other religions and beliefs. Once a story is created, we must live the consequence of that story. The consequence can often be predicted from the details contained in the story we have created.

28. Four Basic Principles

When pain is experienced, whether physical or psychological, do not resist it

When pain is experienced, it must be allowed as long as it is present

When pain is experienced, and while following the above principles, it is important to continue your life as normal. Do not opt out with the idea that you will get back to the process once the pain has subsided

There are exceptions to these rules, do not put your health at risk and do not forget that pain is a sign that something is wrong. Identify, if you can, what is wrong and do something about it. If you find you have done all you can, follow the above principles. It is not necessary to experience extreme states of pain if something can be done to alleviate it.

Understand that, without exception, pain is ultimately the result of believing something to be true that is in fact false

29. How Tight is Your String?

One day, Buddha was watching a musician tuning his instrument. He noticed that when the musician tightened his string too far, the string broke. When the musician did not tighten his strings enough, the instrument was out of tune. From this simple observation, Buddha realised the importance of 'the middle way', a central principle of Buddhism. We are not so dissimilar to the strings of these ancient instruments. If we are wound too tight, we may break, but before that we embody a heightened state of tension. This tension is clearly observable in our bodies and in our behaviour. We become quick to anger and are always on the lookout to find an excuse to vent our anger. The excuse we find has little to do with the anger. Whenever we experience pain, the string begins to tighten. Most of this tightening tends to occur when we are young because we are not able to process the pain that inevitably comes our way. The pain is repressed and therefore held in the body.

Tension is our observable resistance to pain and with this tension, we manifest resistance to life itself. Love is acceptance, but resistance is the opposite of acceptance. When we resist, we cannot truly love. We can create substitutes for love like sex, money, food, alcohol and drugs, but these substitutes can only satisfy us for a short time. Without love, we are hardly even alive. Begin to observe the degree to which you resist. Observe those moments when reality as it is does not suit you; the moments when you either wish that reality was other than it is, or those moments when you do something that is an expression of that resistance. They are the moments when, for instance, we smoke, take drugs, drink alcohol or eat too much. It might also manifest in those moments when we feel angry or express anger towards another. When we criticise or judge, others, this is also an expression of resistance and we are in effect saying they are not behaving or being the way we think they should. This means that we have an idea or image in our heads that is different from the reality we are faced with. In these moments, it becomes clear that we have tried to replace what is with what is not.

When we express the middle way, we become virtually invisible. By definition, it does not contain extremes of any kind. We cannot help noticing the extremes in the world; they demand our attention – that which is not extreme seems to go unnoticed.

The way that news is presented is a good example of this. If it is not extreme, it is not news. We are fed a diet of extremes and we in turn become extreme.

How tight is your string? If you want to find out, sit still in front of a wall with your eyes open for twenty minutes. This should be very easy; for once in your life, nothing is required of you. All you have to do is just sit. This should be easy, but it is not; in fact, it may be the most difficult thing you have ever done. Finding this difficult, we may come to the conclusion that there is something wrong with the meditation rather than there is something wrong with the one who meditates. Meditation is a mirror in which we see the truth of who we are. What we are usually not prepared for is the manner in which the mirror reflects that truth. The mirror does not use words to tell you the truth, it uses feelings or more specifically physical sensations. Pain, for instance, may be one of these physical sensations. You may ask, where is the truth in that? 'Firstly', pain is not the truth, because by the time we have labelled a sensation as pain we have already left the truth behind. If we label a sensation as pain then we have subtly moved away from the truth. It may seem that we have not moved very far, but in fact we have moved as far as it is possible to go. Sensation has no meaning; it is not good or bad, big or small, it is just sensation. It is a truth that arises and then passes away. Giving sensation a name such as 'pain' means that not only is the sensation now more difficult to allow, but that in the future, it becomes more likely we will do the same thing.

In meditation, I experience my inability to be still. Strangely, stillness is seen as the threat and not the fact that my mind is in a state of turmoil. It is unpleasant to sit with this turmoil; surely it is easier to just get up and put the telly on or go for a drink with some friends? There is no doubt it is easier in the short term, but definitely not in the long term. In the long term, my inability to be with myself will cause me to experience many kinds of pain. The inability to be with myself is already a state of pain, but there are mechanisms to alleviate this pain or defer it.

In meditation, we come face to face with the truth of what we are. We become aware that we are not comfortable with who we are without certain props, such as alcohol, cigarettes, drugs, sex and food. Somehow, the fact that we cannot be still and at peace with ourselves seems to go unnoticed. If we did notice this strange state of affairs, we might be in a position to do something about it.

Why I cannot be still is an important question. Perhaps it is boring to be still, but if being still is boring then it would be more accurate to say I am boring and I do not like sitting with that fact. When I can experience the discomfort of feeling what I truly feel, without resistance of any kind, then the conflict at the centre of my being has no need to exist. To be in conflict, there needs to be a disagreement within myself. This could be summed up as 'I am what I am but I would rather that

I was not'. To be in tune requires us not to be in a state of conflict (string too tight). It also requires that there is enough motivation to do this and if there is not (string too loose) then we must wait until we have experienced more pain.

When a musician tunes his strings, he listens with great attention. When he hears discord, he adjusts the string until he can no longer hear the discord. Once the strings are in tune, the musician only has to continue paying attention to the sound the strings make in order to make any additional adjustments that may become necessary.

30. Why Do We Choose Pain?

Why do we choose pain? Most people's response to this question is that they certainly do not choose pain. The problem here is that if we do choose pain but don't know that we do, how could anything ever change? When people say they do not choose pain, they are not lying but nor are they telling the truth. They are not lying, because consciously they really believe they *are* telling the truth. The unconscious mind, however, has an alternate view. It is not a problem for the unconscious mind to choose something that makes no sense to the conscious mind. It is possible for the unconscious mind to choose the absolute opposite of what the conscious mind chooses.

How is it that we can make two totally opposite choices at the same time and not notice?

We could consciously wish to be loved, successful and healthy. The conscious mind can easily believe that it wants these things and that, given time, these things are possible. In the meantime, we may not notice that there is a pattern occurring of constant sabotage.

In relationship, we may find that, although we wish to be loved, we are constantly choosing partners who are incapable of loving. We may say we didn't know our partners would turn out to be like that. This is usually not true. We are usually given all the information we need about our partner within a very short space of time. We give each other many clues about who we are and sometimes we are given direct information. So why don't we notice? We don't notice because we don't *want* to notice. We already have an image in our mind of what we want, so we carefully erase any discrepancies between what we want and reality.

We may wish to be loved, but are we able to love? If we are not able to love then it becomes difficult for others to love us. The reason we choose pain is because our root belief is that we are unlovable. Strange as it may seem, when we have this unconscious belief we can behave in such a way as to prove that this belief is correct. If we believe we are unlovable, it follows that we would behave in unlovable ways. Behaving in an unlovable way, it becomes certain that we will experience the proof we are looking for.

31. Wisdom is the Absence of all Stories

What are we to do? We are born into this life without an instruction manual. We have no idea where we came from, or where we are going, and no idea about what is supposed to happen in between. Naturally, we turn to those who arrived before us with the assumption that they must know what is going on. But of course, these others have not long been here themselves and when they arrived they did exactly what we do; they made the assumption that society, adults and parents were here before them so must know what is going on. This is rarely ever questioned. The ones who do question it are often seen as higher spiritual beings like Buddha or Christ. Just to make matters more complicated, we find that many people are very happy to tell us, in great detail, exactly what is going on. If we ask, how do they know, they may say it came to them in a dream or a vision. Sometimes they say God appeared to them and proclaimed the rules that must be followed.

Because most of these visitations from God occurred hundreds and sometimes thousands of years ago, we accept them on faith. In fact, faith becomes an absolute necessity for these ideas to continue for such a long time. A definition of faith is believing something we do not know to be true. If a scientist were to come along and say 'I have invented a time machine and I have travelled to the distant past or future,' we would, being open- minded, accept this possibility but still require proof. If this scientist were to say 'unfortunately I don't have any proof and my time machine has been stolen, along with the plans to build it,' we might begin to suspect that something is not quite right here.

In the modern world, very little is accepted on faith, yet this tendency from the past lingers on. Wars are fought over competing ideas and horrors are perpetrated in the name of religion. It is not uncommon for psychopaths to declare that God made them or told them to kill, torture and maim. We are like children, willing to accept any fairy story as being literally true, but we are not children and surely this has gone on too long.

We choose all of this rather than accept that we have no idea what is going on. One of the joys of this life for me is the sense of absolute mystery that surrounds the whole of creation. In the very moment when we take on any belief about existence, the mystery that is inherently there is eradicated. The world of the known is a world of boxes with different names, none of which say anything at all. It is dark in a box; there is no light and it is locked – nothing can get in or out. What is in the box can be rearranged, but nothing is actually changed as a result. A coffin is a box; its purpose is to hold dead things, things with the mystery taken out of them. Outside the box is a universe of unlimited possibilities. All creativity takes place outside the box; inside the box there are only dead things.

All that we know or can know is a story. Our parents begin telling us stories as soon as we are born. We may be born into a home where there is much love or little love, but regardless of either of these possibilities, a story is formed and believed. Obviously, we would prefer one story to the other. The story at this point is quite simple; we believe ourselves to be either lovable or unlovable. These two stories are, in my opinion, the two most common stories we can tell ourselves. Of these two, the story that we are unlovable is by far the most widely believed. When asked about our story, we often use other stories to explain the story we have been asked about. For instance, if we ask someone why they believe in God, they will always tell you a story or they may even refer to a book that is full of stories – such as the Bible or the Koran or perhaps a Buddhist text.

All books are about stories. We seem to think some books are based on fact and some on fiction. It would be truer to say that some books appear to be concerned with things that we hold to be true, but as we have seen so many times in the past, what we hold to be true today can be considered ridiculous tomorrow.

As a psychotherapist and meditation teacher, I hear endless stories. I also tell many stories. I have no idea if the stories I tell are true or not, but I am more concerned with using a story to challenge someone's rigidly-held story.

An example is a woman who told me very seriously that she never lies. My response was to say that perhaps she should practise. This created a very interesting response in her; she laughed long and hard in a way I had never seen before. In this case, it was not my intention to replace this woman's story with another story, but to create a paradox that enabled her to loosen up a bit about this very rigidly moralistic stance. Although it might seem like a very good thing to never lie, in this woman's case I believe it was not. The context of this particular story is that this woman's parents were Jehovah's witnesses and her story was crippling her with the idea of perfection.

Even an apparently good story can have unseen negative consequences. The reason for this is that, even though a story may appear to be good, it is nevertheless still a story and a good story can soon become a bad story if it turns out not to be true. Wisdom is the absence of all stories.

32. Doors

In psychotherapy, people tell me their stories. They tell me about their childhood or maybe about what is going on in their lives at the moment. What they talk about is what I consider to be 'blood washing blood', a commentary by the ego about the ego. So what, then, is the point of psychotherapy? It is not that people should not tell me their stories, but what I do with what they tell me. If, for instance, someone tells me they are unhappy in their relationship, I listen to what they say, but what they say is not the point. The point is somewhere behind the words.

Within the words and within the way the words are said, there are doors. These doors lead to other worlds and dimensions. I have no idea where these doors will lead me; I just know they will lead me somewhere. The words someone uses tell me more than the person knows or intends to tell me. They are not only telling me their story, they are telling me their attitude and they are telling my how they view the world. They are also telling me what it is they believe about themselves and their relationships. In knowing what someone believes, it becomes relatively easy to help solve whatever problems they may have. There can be no problem without believing something that is not true. Sometimes the door that appears before me leads to a door within me.

33. Enfoldment

There is no such thing as free will; we do not choose anything. What we take to be our choice is just a thought arising from nowhere that we take to be 'our' choice. Even if you don't believe this to be true, suspend your disbelief for a while and let us conduct an experiment. Accept for now that the thoughts that arise in you are coming from nowhere; they are just arising. When a thought arises that has any trace of conflict in it, such as 'I feel angry', ask yourself a question. The question is, 'is it OK that I am having this thought or this feeling?' In this context 'OK' does not mean good, it means true, so we are asking if this thought or feeling is true or if it is actually taking place.

This is not difficult if we leave judgements aside and just focus on the fact. Am I thinking this thought or not, and is this happening or not? Remember to start off with the assumption that we are not choosing to think or feel.

The process so far is that a thought or feeling arises and we ask whether it is OK or true. After identifying, for instance, that I have had an angry thought and that it is true, another thought may arise such as 'I still feel angry', so the question now asked is, 'is it OK that I still feel angry?' This is what I call 'enfoldment'. Anything can be enfolded, for instance 'I don't like my life', after being identified, may turn into 'I am really unhappy'. We are not getting into a debate with ourselves, just identifying what takes place. Again, we ask whether it is OK to feel really unhappy or true that this is what I am feeling. This in turn may become 'how does that help me?' Now we ask if it is OK that we are now asking, 'how does that help me?' This process can go on indefinitely. Whatever arises, just ask if it is so or if it is ok. Run through this process whenever you can and try to keep it running for a week. Observe what takes place.

What is important here is that we acknowledge the fact of what is taking place, without asking any questions as to why it is taking place or what it means. We begin to develop an interest just in the fact that it is taking place. We can broaden this process to include everything that occurs in life – internally and externally.

It is important to understand that the physical sensations occurring in our bodies largely determine our experience of living. Learn to distinguish the physical sensations as they occur without trying to understand what these sensations mean. We are just looking at the fact of what is happening, while leaving aside any ideas as to why it is happening or what it means. As we learn to do this, we begin to free ourselves from the domination of our own thoughts.

Externally, there is a whole world of movement, sound, colour and light. There are also other living beings. Learn to see this fact without the need to name or describe these beings in any way. This process may be difficult at first, as we are so programmed to add a commentary to what we are experiencing. It is this commentary, more than anything else, that removes wonder and joy from our lives. As with the first part of this process, observe all that is taking place externally with the question 'Is this Ok – is this true?'

Do not analyse what is taking place, just observe the fact of it. As we begin to see more clearly what is actually taking place, the wonder and joy that was lost begins to return.

34. The Ghost

There is a film called *The Others* in which a woman and her children are living in a house that seems to be occupied by ghosts. They hear voices and experience unexplainable occurrences in the house and feel very afraid. It turns out that it is the woman and her children who are the ghosts. The people living in the house produce the unexplainable occurrences. It seems to me that what we take to be reality is not dissimilar to this film; we believe that we are alive and that we are real. The ego is a ghost that believes itself to be living. When the truth is seen, the ghost disappears and in its place a true human being emerges. The ego is an airtight system that can only function so long as it is implicitly believed in. The moment there is a doubt as to the truth of what we hold to be true, a crack occurs in the ego. As doubt grows about the veracity of the ego and its pronouncements, the crack grows bigger and with perseverance will crumble. Once begun and persevered with, this process is inevitable.

There is such a thing as truth, just as there is that which is not truth. The process involves simply distinguishing the difference between true and false. In each moment, there is the possibility of seeing, experiencing and acting from the truth. The truth can be likened to the laws of physics. Without ever thinking about it, we are observing these laws constantly. We have no need to think about these laws, because we know them so well that they are second nature to us. When we learn to walk, ride a bike or drive a car, we are learning about the laws of physics. Learning involves the experience of doing and by doing we come into contact with these laws. As the child learns to walk, he comes into contact with the law of gravity and this contact initially results in failure. In actuality, there is no failure; there is just learning in a very natural and precise sequence. Each time the child falls, learning has taken place that will be added to until there is complete understanding. When there is complete understanding, the child walks efficiently and with confidence and never has to think about how it is done. The child has learned that 'truth' works. In the process he has learned that what is not true does not work. There is no fooling this process, because it either works or it does not.

Without this initial learning we would be unable to walk, talk, eat, work or do any of the things we take for granted in our lives. Once having learned this truth, we feel that we have arrived and no longer need to learn what I would call 'stage one truth.' As a child, we more or less master stage one truth but seem to be unaware of stage two truth. Stage two truth is subtler; so subtle, in fact, that very few ever learn it. The reason for this is that, whereas in stage one truth we are learning about the truth in relationship to the external world, in stage two the learning is about our relationship to who we really are. This is far more problematic; between stage one and stage two, there is a bridge to be crossed. The bridge is the ego and the problem arises because the ego believes that the question of who 'I' really am has already been answered. If this question truly had been answered, there would not be the problems we see around and within us in the world today. From the point of view of the ego, the 'I' and the ego is all there is; they are the same thing. The only reason I can see why this would change would be because the 'I' or the ego are 'not true', and because they are not rooted in truth they do not work. Not working means that inevitably the results of our actions arising from the ego cause pain.

Pain is the clue and the key to finding our way out of the ego's labyrinth. The result of a wrong action is pain, even if that pain does not arise in the moment of the action. In stage one when the child performs a wrong action such as falling, the action and the consequence are close together in time. This helps the child learn faster as the consequence of his action is almost immediate. In stage two the consequence of our action may not occur or be known to us for many years or ever. Smoking cigarettes is a good example of this; we may know that this is a wrong action and that in years to come it may kill us, but the gap between the action and its consequence is so great that it may appear that it does not exist at all.

As the years go by, the consequences of our past actions may begin to catch up with us and the pain begins. The pain should be seen not as a punishment, but rather as a learning process. Even when the pain arising from past actions begins, the learning process is far from easy. In stage two, the problem is not just about the consequence of our actions, but more importantly it is concerned with who is it that experiences pain.

In the beginning, it is unlikely we will arrive at this understanding and we will have to go through the whole ego process of denying and avoiding pain and believing that it is related to something external. All of this is incorrect and in time we may come to see this. If we do see this, we will begin to see more and more clearly that the external world is not the important factor in arriving at truth.

To arrive at the truth, we need to turn our attention back on itself and pose the question of who it is that is attentive to anything, internal or external. Turning our attention back on itself must begin as a result of a movement by the ego. The ego or the 'I' are not based on truth and as such cannot be said to truly exist. It is because of this truth that turning our attention in the right direction allows that which is not true to fall away naturally and easily. It is not 'I' that does this; rather, it is the fact that this possibility lies implicitly within us. Turning our attention back on itself can only occur when there is doubt as to the veracity of the ego. Although we may arrive at a thought such as 'the ego is not real', this is not enough to stop us from continuing to believe that it is. When we turn our attention back on itself consistently, something unexplainable begins to happen.

Ramana Maharshi likened this to seeing a length of rope and mistaking it for a snake; when we move closer to the rope or throw more light on it the truth is seen. As far as our senses are concerned, the seeing of the rope is always the same in that the eyes see *something*. The eyes may see something that resembles a snake that upon closer study turns out to actually be a snake. The problem is not to do with whether or not the rope is a snake or not. The problem is only concerned with identifying the truth. Not seeing the truth, we mis-identify the rope for the snake. Seeing the truth we see the rope as a rope.

35. Reality Check

What is reality? This question may seem profound and almost impossible to answer, or it may seem simple and obvious. I believe the answer is closer to the simple and the obvious. Ask yourself this question right now and, before you begin, take a moment to stop everything – not necessarily externally but internally, just take a moment to be still.

With attention, look at what is taking place where you are right now. Be aware of the posture of your body. Notice the details of the place you are in such as the quality of light. Are there any others in your vicinity? Be aware of any sounds you are hearing; if you can hear someone talking, just be aware of the sound of their voice rather than the meaning of what they are saying. Notice the sensations in your body; again, do not give any meaning to sensations – just be aware that there *are* sensations. When checking reality, it is only necessary to check a few aspects; what is most important is that these few aspects are occurring right now and this can be done very quickly and easily.

Checking reality in this way disrupts the semi-dream state we are normally in. The power of this practice comes when we are able to check reality many times during each day.

The more you do this, the more the semi-dream state is disrupted. In effect, when we check reality, we are moving our attention from what is not true to what is true. Saying something is good or bad cannot be based on truth. Good and bad are value judgements that are layered over the top of reality. When we do this, we fall into the error of believing the part that is layered over reality, rather than the underlying truth of reality. We have been making this error for a long time, building up layer after layer of judgements that we have taken to be true. If this error is not reversed, the outcome can be disastrous. It is also possible that some of these layers are more untruthful than others. The more layers of untruthfulness we accumulate, the more difficult it is to reverse the process.

Recently, I heard someone say that she realised that she was self-destructive and that she was aware that this came about because of the way her mother had treated her as a child.

On one level, this sounds reasonable and I don't doubt that something occurred in this woman's childhood that must account for her belief that she is self-destructive. Nevertheless, when we hold this statement up to the light of reality, we see that there is no truth to this statement whatsoever. It can be very quickly and easily dismissed as being untrue, just by seeing the simple fact that it is about the past. The past is not the present and is therefore not reality. Reality is what is occurring in any given moment. It was very clear to me that, in the moment, this woman was showing no signs of being self-destructive. In fact, she was sitting on a chair, looking very calm and relaxed. When this woman spoke about her mother, I observed that her mother was nowhere to be seen. This may sound ridiculous, but it was nevertheless an observable truth; everything that was being said had no relationship to what was taking place in the present. If this woman had made this statement to someone else, it is quite likely that the other person would comment on this statement by asking a question about what she meant by saying she was 'self-destructive'. If this did happen, the woman would have experienced a confirmation that what she was saying had some basis in truth.

It might be that we do not want to be disturbed in the telling of our story and might even feel angry if someone were to say, as I did, that the story had no basis in reality. But if anger arises as a response to being told something, we have again drifted away from reality. The anger arises because something is being said that we do not want to hear.

What reason could there be for us not wanting to hear someone else's view? It can only be that we have already decided what reality is and that we are not prepared to accept any other version. Anger is, therefore, a clear sign that we believe something that isn't true.

36. The God Realm

For many years, I have likened my human experience to suddenly waking up on a strange planet and not knowing who I am or how I got here. Something about this idea resonates strongly with me. It recently occurred to me that humans are animals that suddenly woke up, in the sense that something occurred in humans that is very different from any other animal. This animal suddenly found it had the ability to reason and, from this power to reason, came the apparent power to choose.

As children, we go through a process that I believe closely mirrors this earlier 'waking up'. I remember a moment very clearly when I was about eight years of age when I was sitting in my family living room. It seems to me now that one moment I was 'asleep' and the next I was 'awake'. Suddenly I was aware of myself and it seemed like a light suddenly came on. With this awareness came choice. Before this, there was awareness without choice. This sudden ability to choose brought with it a number of problems. Awareness without choice is not so very different to the animal state. What is done, is done without conscious awareness of the one who is doing. With this ability to choose, we now seem to think that without choice we would not do anything, so now we need to choose everything.

This reminds me of a time when I suggested to people on a meditation retreat that they focus their attention on their breath. Later, a number of people told me that they became aware that when they focused their attention on breathing they found that they were not breathing naturally, but were subtly trying to control the way they were breathing. Breathing is perhaps the one thing that we do not need to consciously control; we breathe whether we control it or not. In this instance, we are choosing something that actually requires no choice.

Knowing we can choose need not mean that we *should* choose. The child suddenly being able to choose has no knowledge about what is necessary to choose and what is not. The child can be overwhelmed with this sudden responsibility of choice and have no idea how to go about it. Naturally, a process of trial and error begins and we see that some of the choices we make have an unwanted outcome, such as touching something that is very hot. But choice is not just about interacting with the physical world; it is also about interacting with others.

In relationship choice is not so simple, because the possibility of choices is far greater and – it seems, with less direct feedback on the outcome of the choice. For instance, the child finds that if he wants something or wants to avoid something he has the ability to lie. This is a choice, but the outcome of this choice is not so clear to the child. It may be the child is not believed, but he can still hold to the lie and find that sooner or later it is forgotten. It may also be that the child gets away with the lie and gets what he wants or avoids something he doesn't want. Both scenarios leave the child with more or less the same information, which is basically that if he lies he can get away with it. This particular problem may never be resolved over the course of his life. Lying is a very powerful tool to the child; he quickly comes to see that he can look at the world or others in any way he wishes. It is not necessary that the way he looks be based on truth; in fact, it often seems preferable that it is not.

Right here is where most of our problems begin. The way that we look at the world or the way we look at others, and especially the way we look at ourselves, seems to have no rules. We can and do look at the world in any number of untrue or downright bizarre ways. The fact that what we believe is untrue and usually causes us pain seems not to cause us to reconsider the view we have come to. This denial of truth can sometimes be quite extreme. We find that we can do the most appalling things to ourselves or others, see what we are doing and the effect it has and carry right on doing it.

The child has too many choices; in fact, compared to animals, our choices seem infinite. This ability to choose can seem godlike.

We begin to realise that it is possible to choose almost anything. The result of this is that we are seduced by our own power. We enjoy the godlike status it confers on us. Being God is very seductive and it seems not to matter what kind of god we become. Even a bad god can feel like God.

What we see in the world is the result of this abuse of power. If we gave children real guns and ammunition to play with, it would not be long before they were killing each other. Having godlike powers does not require that we are reasonable. It does, however, require that we experiment to find the limits of this power. This seems to me to be what the human race is doing right now. This experimental process is observable in the behaviour of adolescents. What adolescents are doing is attempting to find the limits of their power to choose. As there are usually no guidelines to this process, adolescents invariably begin to conduct a series of experiments. We all do this to some degree and with varying degrees of success. In this period, we feel we can do anything, but at the same time the world may thwart us and we may find that no matter how hard we try we fail to achieve what we desire. We can see that adolescents can be very irritable when they feel they are being thwarted. They are just coming into contact with reality and the laws inherent in reality. When we find that reality does not conform to our expectations of the way it should be, we very subtly adjust reality. If the adolescents' parents do not behave towards them in the way they expect them to, they may become enraged and believe they do this because they are bad parents. They may not consider that their parents are trying to protect them from getting carried away with the sense of being God.

We may feel godlike, but we are always very vulnerable and we need to experiment with some caution. I am not saying we should not experiment, but that we do it with caution. Actually, we must conduct this experiment if we are to complete the cycle and become responsible human beings able to relate, work and have families of our own. If we fail in this, it does not matter how old we get, we will never become true adults. Many adolescents' response to this might be that, looking at the way adults behave, who wants to be an adult?

The adults they are talking about, however, are not true adults – they are adults in body, but not in mind. In mind, they failed to complete the experiment to find the limits of their power. They failed to find the limits of their power because at some point they gave up. This is true of any adult who ingests harmful substances into his or her body. It is true of any adult who chooses to steal, to lie or to harm himself or others. It is also true of someone who believes himself to be depressed, neurotic or to have almost any mental illness.

Doing what we want, when we want, may seem very attractive but there is a problem. One of the results of the experiment undertaken by the adolescent is the understanding that with all actions come consequences. If we pay attention to this fact, we may then go deeper and find precisely what the consequence of our actions might be. Many of us give up on this endeavour and settle for a life of endlessly making the same mistakes and never learning from them. This can be extremely painful and destructive for oneself or for those around us. Fortunately, it is never too late to get back on track and complete this process and it really is better late than never.

At the beginning of this chapter, I mentioned that the choices we make are only apparent choices. Although it is not possible for us to exercise free will and to choose, it is possible for us to believe and to feel that we are choosing. When we come to see that we can choose nothing and that the universe chooses everything, we may become truly godlike.

37. Hell

For me, hell is a repetitive cycle that the mind locks into. This can be summed up fairly simply; pain occurs and the response of the mind is to move away from it. In moving away from pain, we feel that we are in control. Now the pain that we moved away from will be repeated in the future. In moving away from the pain too quickly, we may temporarily ease the pain but the wisdom that was held within the pain is now lost. There is a mechanism in life that causes anything left unprocessed to be repeated until it is processed. Any time we are faced with a problem and decide we would rather not face it, all we are really doing is adding this problem to any other problem we did not want to face. It is like piling up weights on a bridge. With enough weight, the bridge will collapse. Rather than placing weights on the bridge, it becomes imperative that we begin removing weights from the bridge.

Each time a problem is avoided, we are also programming ourselves with the directive that we are weak and fearful and that this is the way it will always be. Processing means giving adequate time and attention to the physical sensations that occur as the problem unfolds. When we are able to give adequate time and attention to these physical sensations, something very interesting occurs; that which we were fearful of is suddenly no longer fearful. At a certain point in this process, wisdom is released. Something very simple is seen that could not have been seen while we were resisting or avoiding pain.

It is as though suddenly there is an overview in which all the parts of the problem are united and the solution becomes obvious. A problem is a problem, as long as it is not seen in its entirety. Avoiding a problem is easy, but also incredibly difficult, as a problem avoided must be faced again in the future with the risk of a breakdown if enough problems are avoided.

This cycle is hell, but it is also the pathway to heaven. We will avoid pain until the realisation occurs that avoiding pain increases pain, and this can only increase so much before a breakdown must occur.

For most people in the world, it seems that this cycle will run until the end of their lives. It does not need to but it will, as these people will never stop believing that they can avoid pain indefinitely.

38. What is Observing What

When I observe the world or any object in the world, what is observing what? Consciousness is that which observes. Without consciousness, there would be no observing anything. If consciousness observes a tree, it is quite clear that what is observing the tree is consciousness, but now let us ask the question, 'what then is the tree?' If there were no consciousness, how could there be a tree or anything else? When we use our senses, such as sight and touch, we seem able to confirm that what is observed is separate from the one that observes – but can this really be so? That which observes is all there is, for without consciousness nothing can be seen to exist. Therefore, consciousness is not only that which observes but that which is observed. In other words, whatever you perceive to be other than you can only be your own consciousness.

All that I perceive, see, hear, touch, taste, smell, think or believe is nothing other than my own consciousness seeing itself. This becomes even more interesting when the question is asked, 'what then is the relationship between that which observes and that which is observed?' This question can be seen to be meaningless, because how could there be a relationship between the consciousness that sees and the consciousness that is seen if both are exactly the same? Relationship requires two separate objects. What is the relationship of water to water? There is none as they are not two. Who has not said 'I do not like him, her or that?' Whenever something like this is said or thought, a paradox occurs; what is actually being said or thought is 'I do not like observing this aspect of my own consciousness.' Right here, it is possible to detect a major lie that we tell ourselves, namely that what is observed is not our own consciousness but something separate from our consciousness. Once this separation has occurred, we become free to hate, lie, kill or to destroy whatever it is we do not like about our own consciousness. This lie is at the heart of all the ills in the world; wars, dishonesty, strife and madness which are the result of self-hatred. That which is hated resides in our own consciousness. Without this self-hatred, there would be love or just consciousness, in all its wondrous forms.

When I say 'our consciousness' or 'my consciousness' I do so in the knowledge that this is another lie that has to be put to rest. If there is such a thing as my consciousness, then the lie is already apparent; 'my' implies something separate from 'your' and this cannot be, because there is no 'my' and there is no 'your'; there is only consciousness. This lie leads to a form of psychosis in which the world and all that is contained in the world, being separate from me, can be used to my advantage. I call this lie 'psychotic', for all the horror that has been perpetrated in its name. All religions and spiritual teachings and all searching for pleasure or power are the means by which consciousness attempts to re-unite with itself. Although in a sense this is natural, it is also impossible for consciousness to search for consciousness. To make matters worse, the desire to re-unite consciousness with consciousness is the very thing that makes it appear as though there is a separation, which is of course the great lie.

Try this experiment: set aside some time, such as an hour, and for that period of time be conscious that all that you see, hear, touch, taste, smell or think is all just consciousness. If any part of that panorama appears to cause discomfort or pain, be aware that pain or discomfort is also just consciousness. Be aware that you and the discomfort are one. It is not really you experiencing discomfort – rather, there is just consciousness in which there is also discomfort. Go further and replace discomfort with sensation; not any particular sensation, just sensation. When we experience discomfort, we usually almost unconsciously slide into a separate reality or a reality of separation. Because we believe who we are is separate from everything else, we apply this same mistaken notion to discomfort or pain. Believing discomfort or pain to be separate from consciousness itself the illusion is created in which there is me and my discomfort.

Both of these are false because there is no me and there is no discomfort; there is only consciousness.

Of course if you believe there is a 'you' and there is 'your' discomfort then you are right. This is the way that consciousness works and whatever you believe to be so becomes so. The belief I am talking about is much deeper than thinking; it is more like the belief in your own identity. It is not something that you think about; it is something that is taken for granted. Believing that I am wonderful sounds like a good idea, but may not be what I really believe. It is what we really believe that determines our reality. There have been many books advocating the power of positive affirmations: believe that you are wonderful and prosperous and it will become so. This is very unlikely, because for most human beings, true belief is more to do with self-hatred than it is to do with being wonderful and prosperous. The only reason we wish to be wonderful and prosperous is because that is precisely what we do not believe we are.

Belief can move mountains but it can also create more horrors than you can conceive of. It is not enough to just believe – it is what we precisely do believe. What you really believe is already manifest. If you believe you are depressed then it is so; if you believe someone has done you harm then it is so, and if you believe your nation is greater than all other nations then it is so. This is so simple and obvious that it seems ridiculous, but it is not. Whatever it is that you really believe is already so. It is not what you believe, but what you really believe.

Look around you and see if it is possible to observe what others believe and if what they believe is so. There is no doubt in my mind that what people really believe is already so, and it is not difficult to see. If someone really believes themselves to be powerful, then that is what they show the world. In the same way, if someone believes themselves to be weak or insecure or afraid, then that is also what is shown to the world and is in fact very hard to hide. Belief can have the same characteristics as a virus; it can spread very fast from one person to another until whole nations are infected. Religious beliefs are like this and so are nationalistic beliefs. This virus aspect can clearly be seen when large groups of people suddenly erupt into violence.

39. One Particular Spot

Many years ago, I came across an apparently true story in a book. I have told this story many times in psychotherapy sessions as it illustrates a number of important principles and it is similar to a parable. The story concerns a psychology lecturer and his students. Having learned a number of psychological principles from this lecturer, his students decide to try an experiment. The goal of the experiment is to influence the lecturer to stand on one particular spot without talking or indicating in any way where that spot might be. Of course, he needs to be completely unaware that this experiment is taking place. How do the students achieve this? The students decide on a predetermined spot before the lecturer enters the room and within a short space of time achieve their objective.

This is how they did it. While the lecturer was talking, the students began showing in certain ways that they were not paying attention; they would talk among themselves, cough, scrape their chairs, and generally show a complete lack of interest unless he happened to stand on the particular spot they had designated. Like most teachers, this man did not feel good about himself if he wasn't seen to be teaching effectively. The only place in the room where he could feel comfortable is on the spot designated by the students. In any other spot, he would begin to feel very uncomfortable. I am sure that in normal circumstances this lecturer would seem a confident and successful man, yet this story illustrates how easily this appearance can change. As long as we are dependent on the behaviour of others for our self-esteem, we leave ourselves vulnerable to this outcome. Ironically, it is vulnerability that is the solution to this problem.

We all are susceptible to this problem of self-esteem, simply by believing something that is not true. This causes us to not feel at ease in our own mind and body. We may appear to be at ease and confident, but this is often a very clever defence. As children, we all learn how to defend ourselves from the criticism of parents, teachers and our peers. We may learn to become very good at this, but below the surface we see that it is not true.

Teachers feel good about themselves if they have a class of well-behaved, attentive students and if they do not get this, they no longer feel good about themselves and may blame the students. This is not because the students cause them to not feel good about themselves, but because they did not feel good about themselves years before they even became teachers. Children are extremely good at recognising whether or not adults feel good about themselves and are very capable of using that information ruthlessly. Teachers and other adults will try to solve this problem in different ways. They may become very aggressive in an attempt to force the children to behave better. They may become secretly vindictive to particular children seeing these children as the instigators or ringleaders. However, none of this will work because the problem is not with the children, it is with the teachers, parents or other adults.

Trying to solve this problem in any way other than in the place where the problem originated is futile. Not feeling good about ourselves is a problem waiting to occur. Not feeling good about ourselves is a secret we hope no one will discover; but this is like pretending we are dressed when we are in fact naked; everyone can see. The first step in feeling good about yourself is to see clearly that you don't; don't try to pretend that you do. This is a bit like lying; the more you lie, the more complicated it gets and the harder it becomes to keep track of each lie. Once the complication of dishonesty is out of the way, there is hope for solving this problem. The next step involves asking yourself a question; 'what is it that tells us that we do not feel good about ourselves?' Strangely, when you look closely at this, you find it is *you* that tells yourself that you do not feel good about *yourself*. Having done this with the mind, the body will confirm this belief by creating physical sensations of discomfort.

This whole structure is always created in childhood, where the possibilities of experiencing failure are everywhere. Failure is first experienced in someone else's eyes and, if experienced enough, becomes failure in our own eyes. It does not take much for parents, teachers, or others children to project failure onto the child.

At no point is any child a failure, because children are in the process of learning and some learn fast whilst others learn slowly. This would only be a problem for parents, teachers or other children who do not feel good about themselves.

We must recognise that we are telling ourselves stories that started off by being told to us by someone else. All that is required is the conscious recognition that the story, regardless of who first initiated it, is just a story that in no way relates to anything true. The next step is to fully embrace the physical sensations that arise whenever we tell ourselves we are not good enough. Trust that if you can fully embrace these physical sensations, they will dissolve of their own accord. 'Fully embrace' means to do nothing, because sensations are just sensations and nothing needs to be done with them. The whole problem is that we will not leave them alone.

What instructions do you need in order to do nothing? Doing nothing does not mean ignoring, because ignoring is doing something. Doing nothing does not even mean paying attention to them, as this is still doing something. The thing that requires the least effort is doing nothing. This is true meditation; just see that everything is as it is and that nothing needs to be done. Everything at all times has always been just as it is. Most of the time, nothing needs to be done because the world is as it is and it is complete. Problems arise when we begin trying to fix something that is not broken. Be aware that most of the time nothing needs fixing; any idea that something does need fixing arises in our mind and has no basis in reality.

I am not referring here to the everyday practical things that need doing, like working, travelling, cooking and washing. The practical things of life fall into a separate category and are usually straightforward; with walking, each step naturally follows the last step taken and no complicated thinking is required. All life is practical and, although this may sound strange, all life is just taking place the way it should. No matter how hard you try the world is as it is and cannot be changed. When we do try to change things, there is no time when the world is still not as it is. We just tell ourselves stories about how we have changed something and what that means.

What needs to be done is practical and is therefore not complicated; this is not to say we cannot make it complicated; just that the nature of doing practical things is actually not complicated.

If you really have the power to change things, make the next moment perfect in all regards and apply this to all subsequent moments. The only way to actually achieve this is by literally doing nothing. When we stop interfering with the world, it begins to reveal itself in all its majesty and what is revealed is consciousness itself. There is nothing you can ever see, hear, touch, taste or think about that is not just consciousness itself. In this moment I am in the mountains of Crete, the sun is going down and the mountains are changing colour in every moment, dogs are barking and the birds are singing. A warm breeze caresses my body and suddenly there is the sound of a motor scooter, and all of this can only be consciousness itself. To say it is my consciousness is saying more than needs to be said; there is just consciousness. To say this is a pleasant experience is saying more than needs to be said. Its not that it isn't a pleasant experience – it's just that it does not change anything by saying it. In consciousness, we are always in the right spot.

40. Punishment

Punishment, like intolerance, is a human characteristic that is not exactly our most endearing trait. We want to punish and we need to punish – sometimes ourselves and sometimes others. Punishment falls into two groups; those who punish openly and those who make the punishment of themselves and others a closely guarded secret. The means of punishment are many and varied. The favoured means of punishment of the human race is withdrawal. This is easy and can be very subtle as we can adjust it to just the right level of effectiveness. We can withdraw attention, money, sex and love. When we withdraw one of these from someone, that person is aware that something is missing but is often unable to express precisely what that is – therefore it remains a secret to all concerned. If it is expressed, it can easily be denied or excuses can be made.

Fear is another favoured means of punishment and again can be used openly or in secret. I worked with a couple some years ago, as a couple, but also individually. The wife told me that she was afraid of her husband; that he had so many rules and she was constantly afraid of breaking one of them. When I talked to the husband about this, he was shocked because he had not realised his wife, and probably others, were afraid of him. He is obviously creating a situation in which his wife and others become afraid of him but somehow he manages to keep this secret, not consciously but semi-unconsciously. He did not deny that he was making his wife afraid of him and even volunteered that others were also afraid of him. Although he wanted this aspect of his behaviour to be kept secret, some part of him knew what he was doing.

Punishment can manifest individually, in groups, nations and even groups of nations. We may be aware of this need or we may not. It is more likely that we are not as this trait is not something most people could feel comfortable with. The cause of us needing to punish ourselves is that usually at some point or maybe many times we have felt punished ourselves. Not knowing how to deal with this, we inwardly decide to pass this punishment on to anyone who is willing to be punished.

At the same time as long as it seems necessary to punish others it cannot be avoided that we will also punish ourselves.

There is no justification for punishing anyone, but this does not mean that there is not a reason why we do this. In my work as a therapist, I find that for most of the people I work with, the idea that they may be punishing themselves or others is the most difficult to take. Yet if we are unable to see this aspect of ourselves, we must inevitably continue to punish. Two questions arise here; 'who do we really want to punish' and 'why?' The person we usually want to punish is not the person we are punishing. Many women need to punish men and many men need to punish women. The way a woman punishes a man will be slightly different in form to the way a man punishes a woman. As I said before, most punishment involves the withdrawal of something from someone. We can withdraw attention, or love, or sex, or money. At some point, this is not enough and our withdrawal becomes more extreme; we separate completely or even resort to violence. These more extreme strategies are really just more extreme means of withdrawal.

When we punish, it is necessary that we remain unconscious of what we are doing. The reason for this is that to be conscious of what we are doing involves seeing that the one we are punishing is not the one we really want to punish. We punish because we have been hurt, and when we are hurt someone has taken power away from us. It is in the nature of the mind that this cannot be tolerated, especially when the hurt was inflicted intentionally. Having lost power in this way, we are compelled to regain this power that is perceived as lost. It is also in the nature of the mind that we do not care how we regain this power. We do not care who we punish for this hurt and loss of power.

A bully is someone who has been hurt, but he or she will rarely try to punish the one who caused the hurt. Usually, the bully will look for a victim preferably someone who will not fight back. To think that it is simply that we are bullies or victims is not true. At different times, we can all become bullies or victims. It is interesting to ask a bully 'why do you want to hurt me?' I have done this a number of times in the past and there is always a look of shock on the person's face.

Why is this? The reason for the look of shock is that the bully somehow believes that what they are doing is a secret. It needs to be a secret to the bully as well as to the victim. No one wants to know that they are a bully, so these impulses to hurt someone needs to be kept secret – even from the victim.

Hurt can be physical and it can be mental. Sometimes, as in the case of sexual hurt, it is both. It seems to be universal that once we have been hurt, our brains become wired in such a way that we are compelled to pass this hurt on. We all know that it is not nice to hurt others, but if we have been hurt, this need exists. Knowing it is not nice to hurt, yet having the need to hurt, it becomes imperative that we find someone to hurt in secret.

The strange thing is that most people seem willing to keep this a secret.

It is as though we collude with each other to play the roles of bully or victim. I see this bullying and playing the victim everywhere. Children do it to other children, parents do it to children and to each other and bosses do it to their employees. As individuals we do it, and we also do it in groups – especially in terms of race.

If we have been hurt, anyone can become fair game. Ask yourself if you have you been hurt. Is there anyone in your life that you punish in any way? Does anyone punish you? You may prefer to keep these things secret, but if that is the case there will be no end to this. The fact that we have been hurt in the past requires that this hurt is processed.

When we pass the hurt on to someone else, we really do this as an attempt to avoid the pain that is in us. This pain cannot be passed on and we can only delude ourselves temporarily that we have passed the pain on. Pain needs to be experienced as physical sensations in the body. This is vulnerability; the ability to feel physically precisely what we do feel. Look around you and allow yourself to see the punishment that goes on between men and women, individuals, groups and nations. Put an end to the secret.

41. All There Is, Is Dreaming

I have come to see that whatever I dream about myself or the world fits precisely with my experience in the world. This raises some very interesting questions. Is there a time when this is not the case? Is it an absolute truth that no matter what I dream that is what I will experience? For me, the spiritual life has always had an attraction even when I was unaware of any spiritual life. In my dream, I see that there are many preferences. I see these preferences as being particular to my dream.

I am writing this chapter in Tiruvannamalai in India. Many of the children in this area appear to be happier, more relaxed and joyful than many of their counterparts in the west. I know that for the first eight or nine years of my life, this was also the case. Then that joy was lost and sometimes replaced with a vision of hell. Once I have a vision of hell, I am compelled to live it. This vision is a dream that is constructed from my misunderstanding of who I am. If I misunderstand myself to be lacking something then that is what I will experience, and that is what the world will see. In my school years, I experienced bullying and I began to build a wall around myself as protection. I began to distrust the motives of others who often seemed to want to hurt me. Over the years, this vision has dissolved. Now when I look at the world, I look at myself. The world appears to be devoid of meaning. I do not mean this in any negative way; just that meaning for me equals dreaming and a dream will always be just that – a dream.

I began this chapter with the intention of answering a particular question for myself.

The question is whether there is anywhere where the dream is not? For instance, it is said that people like Ramana Maharshi came to realise their true self. What if what he realised was just another dream about having a true self? Is it possible that this true self is also just another dream? The answer must be that it is possible. How can we ever know what someone else's experience is? Again, the answer must be we cannot know; we can only believe.

This seems to me to be a very important question. When I look around me, I see everyone inhabiting his or her own particular dream. Some of these dreams are visions of hell.

What we believe is what we dream. The possible variations of what we believe are endless. When I look at the world, this is precisely what I see. As a psychotherapist, I get to see in more detail exactly what people are capable of dreaming. Whatever it is they believe or dream, that is what they are compelled to live. Visions of hell can be very subtle and may appear on the outside to be visions of heaven. For instance, we may find that we have all that we desire such as a good job, a beautiful wife/husband/children and a lovely home. Let us assume you have all these things and you are perfectly happy. Now imagine that due to unforeseen circumstances, you lose all these things. Would your dream still be a dream of heaven? If the answer is yes, then you are a rare individual. For most, there would be a major collapse and their dream of heaven would quickly turn to a dream of hell.

Every year there are stories of people killing themselves because they are in debt. They may not be poor, but they are no longer rich. They are still healthy and often they have families that love them, yet still they kill themselves. Actually, almost any change in our circumstances can change our dream in disastrous ways. The reason for this is to do with dependency and expectations. Both of these are aspects of dreaming. When our happiness is dependent on something or someone, it means that our happiness is an illusion. The illusion is revealed when we lose that which we are dependent upon. When we have expectations of how life should be and we find life does not fit with these expectations, we begin to suffer. The degree to which you will suffer is dependent on the degree of your expectations.

All of this is dreaming and what we dream is what we must experience. So I come back to my original question; is it possible to stop dreaming? There are two apparent answers to this question: yes and no. It is only in the world of dualistic thinking that this answer is a paradox. We may think about the world in a dualistic way, but this does not mean that the world itself is dualistic. The reason it is not possible to stop dreaming is that so long as we inhabit a living body, we must experience consciousness.

Through the body and its senses, we experience the world and the whole of this experience manifests as consciousness. This experience, however realistic it may seem, is a dream. What you see and what you experience is largely determined by the nature of our bodies. I assume that if you had the body of an insect, this dream would be a different dream.

The reason it is possible to stop dreaming is because our dreams are mostly determined by our beliefs and beliefs of any kind are illusory. Take the statement 'I believe in God' expressed in words which, right now, are just pixels on a computer screen. At some point, these words may appear as ink on paper, but at no time are they any more than that. These words may take the form of a thought, so what then are they formed of? Whatever they are formed of, the brain gives them no more meaning than pixels on a screen or ink on paper. In each of these examples, what gives these words life and apparent meaning is our belief in them. The fact that we believe our own beliefs really tells us nothing. Because this is true, it follows that it must be possible to realise this so that we no longer see the world through the lens of our beliefs.

42. Why Do I Want This?

What is it we want? Everyone in the world seems to want something; they seem to be consistently unhappy that they haven't got it, and rarely happy with what they do have. What if we already have what we want, and that this has always been the case and always will be? What are you doing right now? I assume that part of what you are doing right now is reading this. Is this something you want to do? Again, I must assume that it is. What are you wearing? Again I must assume that it is what you want to be wearing. If you make yourself a cup of tea, I assume that this is because you want to and that you want tea rather than coffee – or any other drink. Whatever it is you are doing you must be doing because you want to, unless someone is holding a gun to your head and forcing you.

Prove to yourself that what you are doing right now can only be what you want to be doing, and even inactivity is doing something. If this is true, it must also be true that everything you have ever done in the past must also have been what you wanted to do. If this is true, it follows that this will always be the case. It is not just that we always do what we want; what we see, hear and understand is also what we want. This part is harder to understand and harder to prove. Whatever we experience can only be known through belief and whatever it is we believe we must want to believe. Regardless of how beliefs come to be formed, it must be true that if we have a particular belief, it must be that we want to have a particular belief. It is not possible for someone to force us to believe anything. Ultimately, we can only believe what we want to believe.

What we feel can be divided into two parts. The first part is what we physically feel – the physical sensations experienced by the body. The second part is what we believe these physical sensations mean. What we feel, therefore, is really what we believe. If you could remove the belief part of what you feel, there would just be physical sensation and without belief there is no meaning inherent in physical sensation. Everything that we experience in life can only be known through what we believe. What we believe is what we want to believe, and everything in life turns out to be what we want.

What we experience is what we want to experience, even when this includes depression or pain. If we are experiencing pain, then crazy as this at first seems, it is because that is precisely what we want to experience.

When I began working as a psychotherapist, I started to notice that people would often complain of suffering in certain ways and at the same time appear to do everything in their power to maintain this suffering. The desire to suffer is rarely a conscious desire. The conscious mind would find it very disturbing to realise that it desires suffering. The unconscious mind, however, has no such problem with this desire. It is useful to view the unconscious as a very safe place to hide our most intimate secrets; so secret that we would rather not know what they are. To know what these secrets are would be to reveal and acknowledge how crazy we are. It is not a bad thing to acknowledge how crazy we are; in fact, it is absolutely necessary if we are to find sanity.

Part of what I am saying is to do with the power of language. Certain words have an incredible power that other similar words do not have. Want is one of those words. Saying that we create our own reality is true enough, but knowing this changes nothing. Using the word 'want' in relation to what we experience forces us to be responsible for our own experience of reality and not invent false beliefs to explain away what we do and what we experience. This is a slightly different angle on quantum theory. Instead of 'we create our own reality', it becomes, 'what we experience is the proof of what we want to experience'. If you are able to accept this and apply it constantly, it is like looking into a magic mirror in which everything we see is the absolute truth. In this way, it becomes impossible to lie to ourselves as to why we are experiencing what we are experiencing. We cannot control this with the intellect and all that is possible is that we keep looking in the mirror, because this looking changes everything.

The ego is a defence system designed to want that which causes us pain, but the real defence is to deny that knowledge. How could we possibly want to suffer? Seeing the truth that what we experience is what we want to experience, this lie is revealed.

Because it is a lie the foundation of the ego disappears and like the 'Wizard of Oz', turns out to be a weak and helpless old man, a fake.

If you look carefully at what you want, you will see that sometimes what you want is what you really *do* want. At other times, you will notice that what you want does not feel comfortable. The reason that what you want may not feel comfortable is because in this case, what you want is connected to a negative belief. For instance an alcoholic, wants to drink and some part of him or her does not feel completely comfortable with this. The negative belief in this case revolves around not feeling good enough. As a result, the alcoholic finds a way to punish him or herself. The ego translates not feeling good enough to 'I have done something wrong and deserve to be punished.' Believing we have done something wrong is buried in the unconscious. Unconscious or not, it is still a belief and is therefore not true.

The proof of what you want is in what you are experiencing in each moment. If you observe what you want in each moment, begin to notice when you are in agreement with what you want. If you are not completely comfortable with what you want, just observe this. Begin to move towards complete agreement with what you want. When there is complete agreement with what you want, everything unfolds easily and without effort. You can have almost anything you want – but be aware that if you want something for the wrong reason, you may get more than you bargained for.

43. What is Wrong With Consciousness?

What is consciousness? The definition of the word 'conscious' is knowing – privy to knowledge and inwardly aware. These definitions are reasonable, but do not go far enough and give us no idea of what consciousness really is. This is not surprising, as it is almost certain that what consciousness really is, is unknowable. Science is never able to say anything about the true nature of anything, but is able to describe much about the behaviour of things. I will not try to explain what consciousness really is but I will try to explain how it works.

If there were no body, could there be consciousness? If we leave belief out of this question, then the answer is that there could be no consciousness without a body. Any body will do – animal, insect or any other kind. The consciousness experienced by any creature will be determined largely by the type of body the creature has. Each body has a degree of consciousness appropriate to the needs of that body. In the case of humans, the degree of consciousness is appropriate to what we do. Without consciousness, there is nothing. Consciousness is all that can be known, no matter how the knowing takes place. That is, when our senses perceive anything, the perception itself is a kind of knowing. This is important as any kind of knowing must be the result of belief. If I look at a tree and don't think about it, what do I see? What I see can no longer be called a tree as the word 'tree' exists as a thought. What I would see cannot be described or named as that would involve thinking, but even so something is seen. The fact that something is seen is the same as saying something is known. If this is so, then what is known can be termed 'a belief'. This belief is much more subtle than the concept of 'tree', yet still this knowing can only exist as belief. If we could take all knowing away, there could be no consciousness.

Consciousness itself is nothing more than belief. It is composed of many layers of belief that range from the impossibly subtle to the point where something is absolutely defined as existing, like a tree. A belief has no independent existence in the world.

Without a body, there can be no consciousness and without consciousness there can be no belief. I have no idea why there is a body or why there is consciousness; only that it is so.

As a child, I remember asking 'How does all this come to exist?' and 'Did it have a beginning and will it have an end?' I did not know it then, but these questions could only arise out of consciousness and could only be about consciousness. All that exists as the universe or the one that is aware of the universe can only be consciousness. Born into this world with the particular body we have, consciousness arises. Having a body, the first priority of consciousness is to survive long enough to procreate. Is survival and procreation the only purpose of consciousness? There are clues to this question that show that survival and procreation are not the only purpose. We need to survive and procreate so that our species lives long enough to solve the real purpose of consciousness. If our species does not live long enough to solve this then another species will arise – if not here on earth, then somewhere else in the universe. The clues I referred to earlier are contained within consciousness and the fact of consciousness itself.

Within consciousness the biggest clue to its purpose is pain. It is as though consciousness were created in such a way as to appear absolutely seamless; seamless, in the sense that from within consciousness, everything in the universe appears separate – especially the observer, me. Not only does it appear separate, but it all seems to fit logically together. This logical fit can only occur through the ingenious invention of time. Time does not exist independently of an observer; it is a measurement that requires someone to do the measuring for it to exist. Consciousness itself is time, as consciousness is knowing and knowing is belief, and belief can only exist with time or measurement. A belief is a measurement because it could not occur without time. Thought occurs in time and has duration; it has a beginning and an end. If it did not, it could not exist. In the space between two thoughts is nothing, or non-existence. Thought itself has no independent existence as a body is required for thinking to occur.

Thought without belief is the same as non-existence. It is belief that supports thinking. Without belief, thinking is like clouds that drift across the sky.

The existence of clouds is dependent on water, light and most importantly belief. Pain is a belief that hurts. Within consciousness, pain is very useful but its true purpose is to reveal that what we believe is not true. Pain will never let you escape this fact until the belief that pain is dependent upon is seen to be untrue.

Ultimately, all that appears to exist within consciousness is unsatisfactory and this is another way of saying it is ultimately painful. All things arising in consciousness must ultimately lead us to suffering. We are driven by desire to obtain that which we believe will make us happy. Even if we are able to satisfy our desires, we find that happiness is very fleeting and the moment we obtain it, we are already looking for something else.

Suffering should result in questioning what we believe. If we do not question what we believe, suffering must inevitably continue. If we do begin to question what we believe, and especially if we question belief itself, then suffering can end.

It is in the fact of consciousness itself that we see another clue that survival and procreation are not its only purpose. Anything that exists must have an origin; therefore if there is consciousness, there must be an origin to consciousness. Consciousness can never find this origin directly as the origin is not itself consciousness. How do we come to understand something? If we try to teach a young child language or maths, we find that it is only at a certain stage of development that this becomes possible. This holds true in regard to understanding anything. Another way of putting this is that we can only understand when we are ready or able to understand. If we are not ready, there is nothing on earth that could make this happen. Wanting to understand and trying to understand is not enough; certain conditions have to occur for this to happen. This is true in regard to anything within consciousness and especially in regard to understanding its origin.

Consciousness cannot understand its origin, it can however understand the implication of the absolute behind it. Trying to understand this before we are ready is impossible, and we will always make the same mistake of looking for the solution within consciousness. This is not to say we will not find solutions; only that they can never be true.

There are many conditions that need to be met for understanding to take place, but there is one condition that seems to me to be the most important. This is that all beliefs must die and they can only die when they are seen to be untrue. This is ironic, as most people are looking for something to believe in – because they believe that who or what they are is not good enough.

Religion, therapy, yoga, meditation or any other kind of self-help are all attempts to solve the problem of not feeling good enough. Because all of these are based on false beliefs, there is no hope. This is not a popular message, but that is not the point. Is it true?

The root meaning of the word 'belief' is to make palatable to oneself. Pain is not palatable; even mild discomfort is not palatable. Boredom is not palatable. Hearing something that does not conform to what you believe is definitely not palatable, especially if it is to do with belief itself.

Here are some simple questions about consciousness. If you enquire into and answer these questions honestly, you will come to see that without any doubt there is nothing wrong with consciousness; there never was nor ever could be. What is wrong with consciousness? Nothing, except the beliefs that arise within it. Can consciousness be more than it is? Can consciousness be less than it is? Can anyone else's consciousness be any different from your consciousness? Does diet affect consciousness? Does meditation affect consciousness? Does being male or female affect consciousness? Does age affect consciousness? The only thing that can affect consciousness is the body dying.

Is there anything wrong with consciousness? Absolutely not – unless you think there is. Consciousness is the gift that comes with the body when we are born. Consciousness is all that is. Imagine a fish in the ocean, asking what the nature of that which I swim in is.

Consciousness is our guide to the absolute; it arises from the absolute. As it arises from the absolute, it is not different from the absolute. The absolute is implied in consciousness. Without belief, consciousness merges with the absolute.

If you understand this, you will understand that consciousness can never be more than it is, no matter what you do.

If nothing you do can affect consciousness in any way, what is it you need to do? It is not wrong to meditate or practice yoga, but none of this can change consciousness in any way. What is it you dislike about consciousness? What you dislike is only what you have come to believe, but what you believe only arises in consciousness. Consciousness does not change as a result of what you believe; it is not affected by anything except the death of the body. With the death of the body, there is only the absolute.

44. How Do you Know if you are Awakened?

Is there such a thing as awakening? Although I have asked and wondered about this question before, I have never asked it in the way I ask it now. In the past, I assumed that there was such a thing as awakening because I had seen in my own mind such big shifts in consciousness that my assumption was that if this continued eventually, 'I' would arrive at this state of awakening or what many call 'enlightenment'. This seems a natural enough assumption to make, as many different kinds of changes occur naturally in all of us as we move from childhood to adulthood, but my assumption contained a very big jump from changes in consciousness to this ultimate state of consciousness referred to as 'awakening'.

How do you know if you are awakened, is the crucial question? Even more important than whether there is such a thing as awakening. It seems to me that the only possible answer to this question must be, 'apart from believing it is so, I cannot know.' You could say you feel it to be so, but the question how do you know, still applies? You could say that it is a deep inner knowing beyond thinking, but still this question applies. To know something, it is necessary to believe something. Because belief can only ever be a preference, knowing must also be a preference. We cannot know; we can only believe. Why would we want to believe there is such a thing as awakening? If I ask myself that question (as I have had this belief for most of my life), I would say that it is because I believe I experienced a brief awakening a number of times when I was young and this was unlike any other experience. It was a very pleasurable experience, and as with all pleasurable experiences, I wanted more of it. Also, if I am awakened, I assume that that means I become someone important and respected, or even venerated. This is all very seductive, but in no way answers this question 'how do I know if I am awakened'. Because I want to be and find the idea pleasant, is not good enough. It also seems clear to me now that wanting awakening and having ideas about what this is and what it would give me must be the one thing that stops it from happening (assuming that there is such a thing in the first place).

I can never know if I am awakened, because any knowing must involve a knower and a believer.

The next question that arises is 'why do so many people claim to be awakened?' Not just in the present, but throughout the past such as Buddha, Jesus, and others. I have to question them the same way I question myself; namely, why would they want to be awakened? They get to be important and respected and even venerated. They also tend to get many followers or disciples who dote on every word they utter and look at them as though they were God incarnate. These followers often make sure that they never want for anything. They may even get to be seriously rich and powerful. They may also get to become very attractive to the opposite sex. Clearly, this whole idea of awakening opens up a minefield of contradictions.

If it is seen clearly that I cannot possibly know if I am awakened, then surely there is nothing to be done, no questions left to ask, and no searching for someone to follow who will lead me to this desirable state. This itself would be the end of the neurosis of believing there is something wrong with me. Of course, it would also be neurotic to think or believe I am awakened, especially if we consider all the many benefits this might give us. If we need to feel more important, this can only be because we don't.

Many seem to believe that you can tell if someone is awakened, because they laugh and smile a lot. Clearly, many followers believe this because they often seem to mimic this behaviour. People who laugh and smile a lot when there is nothing in particular to laugh or smile about could also be a little crazy. There is no behaviour that can tell us if someone is awakened or not. People often think that if you are awakened, you would also be very compassionate and loving, but this also proves nothing. I have met many people in my life who are naturally very compassionate and loving and none of them claim to be awakened. Words of wisdom might be another sign of whether we are awakened or not; anyone interested in awakening can usually do the necessary homework. There is no shortage of books or teachers from which to study.

Throughout history, people have looked at the behaviour of teachers like Buddha and decided that mimicking his behaviour will produce the same results. Mimicking means pretending, but how can pretending anything ever lead to something true? If only it were that easy. For me, if there is such a thing as awakening, it cannot be linked to any neurotic desire to be awakened or to believe that there is something wrong with us that we should need this. What is wrong is only that we believe there is something wrong; if we did not believe this, there would be no desire to proclaim oneself or anyone else as being awakened.

Many years ago in America, Houdini set out to prove once and for all if it was possible to contact the dead. At that time, there were many who claimed this ability. Being a master illusionist himself, he was able to figure out how this supposed contact was made. There was not one instance in which he found he could not prove conclusively that there was some form of trickery taking place. Many thousands of Americans wanted to believe that this was possible; because they could not deal with the reality of losing someone they loved. These people were very willing to part with large sums of money to see and hear this evidence that their loved ones lived on in a better place. This is not so dissimilar to thinking that there is something wrong with you and being willing to do anything to bring about this magical transformation that will at last make you truly important. If any of what I have written offends you, then I would urge you to question why this is. There is no doubt in me that if something hurts or offends you, it must be because you believe something that is not true. If what you believe is true, why would anything offend you? It can only offend you because you would like to believe something for reasons such as I have stated above. When someone informs you that what you desire is based on a false belief, this naturally hurts because what you believe is just that, a belief, and no belief can ever be true. Some part of you knows this as you must have experienced the collapse of so many other false beliefs in your life.

There has always been a great need in all of us to believe in and hope for something more. This 'more' could be God, everlasting life, awakening, enlightenment, money or power.

It is clear to me that all these false beliefs are the cause of the suffering, wars and insanity we see in the world around us. If there is such a thing as love, it must be in the absence of these false beliefs that it can arise.

45. If Thine Eye Offend Thee Pluck it Out

Consciousness arises from the absolute and all that can be known arises from consciousness. The absolute cannot be known directly, but its implication is everywhere. We cannot see the air we breathe, but we can see the implication of air in the breeze and its effect on leaves and grass and all living creatures. We cannot see gravity, but again the implication of gravity is everywhere. Consciousness is whole; it is not formed of parts. What we experience as parts is not unlike an optical illusion. What is seen as separate objects is very convincing, but these separate objects can only exist with consciousness. What we see is a representation of something. When we look at a tree, we see light that is reflected from the tree into our eyes and brain. In the brain, this light is processed and translated into an image of something that is then labelled as a tree. The whole of this process is a truly miraculous trick of consciousness. The same trick occurs when sound- waves enter the ears or physical sensations enter our body through the nerve endings in our skin. This is data that is processed and translated by the brain and the mind into all the things that we can experience. As in a mirage, water may be seen but can never be tasted.

Is the observer different from that which is observed? When I look at a tree, there is the observer; me and the tree the observed. The observer, me, is conscious and in my consciousness I see a tree. This tree is not separate from my consciousness, and in fact cannot exist except through my consciousness. All that can ever be experienced can only be my own consciousness. We would all probably agree on the form of the tree we are seeing, but think of all the different ways we may experience the tree. We may see the tree as a thing of beauty or indifference. We may see it as useful, as a source of wood, fruit, shade, money or air. The way we see a tree is particular to our own consciousness. Even what is visually seen is particular to our own consciousness. If you apply this reasoning to the way we experience each other then you can begin to see why the world is in such a mess. We can only experience our own consciousness and all that we experience is that consciousness.

In effect, when I hate someone what I actually hate is my own consciousness. This obviously also holds true of any other emotion I may feel. Hatred or love are conditional on the experiences of my life. If I have experienced much love in my life, then it is natural that I experience the world and others in a more loving way than someone who has experienced hatred and violence. Having experienced hatred or love, these feelings are projected onto others. We do not do this because they deserve it, but because something within consciousness has become conditioned to do this. When someone kills, they are killing that which they hate in their own consciousness. Racism or sexism can only exist in someone who hates their own consciousness. This is the meaning of 'if thine eye offend thee pluck it out'. What offends you can only be a part of your own consciousness and plucking out your eye will not help. It is not what the eye sees that offends you; it is the one who sees that is looking for something to be offended by. Nothing can actually be plucked out, but we can come to see that what we love or hate is only our own consciousness.

There is no 'my' consciousness or 'your' consciousness; there is only consciousness. Consciousness that is seen as belonging to me or you is not itself different. What is different is that the things contained in my consciousness have been processed very differently than the things contained in your consciousness. It is because of this separation of 'me' and 'you' that all the problems in the world arise. Consciousness itself is pure; it has no beliefs and does not discriminate.

Zen master Bankei referred to consciousness and the implication of the absolute as the unborn Buddha mind. It is referred to as 'the unborn' because the origin of consciousness is the absolute, and the absolute is without cause. It has no beginning and no end. Because the origin of consciousness is the absolute, it is not different from the absolute.

Believing consciousness to be composed of parts the implication of the absolute is hidden. Without belief and therefore without parts, consciousness is pure and unchanging. Abiding in pure unborn consciousness, the implication of the absolute is revealed.

46. Seeing The Light

Light from any object, no matter from how far or how close, arises in the mind virtually instantaneously. This light is processed by the brain and mind and organised into the world we see and experience. This applies equally to sound or any other form of information. We do not see objects such as stars in the distance we see them in our own brain, mind, and consciousness. The universe is being created in each moment in our consciousness. The light we see represents something as it was in the past, but the light itself occurs only now. Most of what we see is reflected light that began its journey, sometimes millions of years ago and sometimes milliseconds, ago but all of it arrives at exactly the same time – now. Light travels at approximately 186,282 miles per second. It takes approximately 8 minutes for the light from the sun to reach your eyes. At no time is it possible to see the sun as it is now; we are always seeing it as it was 8 minutes ago. It can take many millions of years for the light from some stars to reach your eyes. Some of these stars are already dead by the time their light reaches our eyes. Light enters the eyes and the brain, where it is translated into an approximation of the object that reflected the light, or the source of the light itself. The universe out there is not out there and it is not in here (in the brain or the mind) but an approximation of it is.

Talking about light and the process that goes on in our consciousness gives no sense of the miracle that is occurring. All that can be seen and known in the universe is being created in each moment in consciousness. Saying something is seen and known seems to imply that there is someone who sees and knows. This is not the case, because that which sees and knows is the same as that which is seen and known. There is only consciousness and, by implication, the absolute. Believing that what is seen is separate from the one who sees, all the horrors and wonders of the world are created. Seeing the truth, the wonders remain but the horrors disappear. If everything and everyone is only an aspect of your own consciousness. what is there to hate?